CONTENTS

Photographic credits

Edimédia: pages 2/3. Giraudon: pages 16, 21, 45, 48, 56, 67, 70, 71. Roger-Viollet: pages 20, 54, 55. Bulloz: pages 48, 57, 60, 65. Erich Lessing/Magnum: page 61. Barbey/Magnum: page 69. Réunions des Musées Nationaux (Musée du Louvre): pages 45, 64, 66. Louis Frédéric: page 68. François Saint-Bris: page 69.

Series directed by Noël Bosetti and Michel Pierre, professors of history with the assistance of Élisabeth Sebaoun.

Guillaume Le Textu (1509–1572), born in Le Havre, was a navigator and cartographer who drew a *Universal Cosmology, according to navigators both ancient and modern* in 1556. Whether of America or Europe, his maps are among the most detailed of the period.

Pierre Desceliers (1500–1558), parish priest of Arques and celebrated scholar, hydrographer, and cartographer, made this planisphere in 1546 by order of King Henry II of France.

HAMISH HAMILTON CHILDREN'S BOOKS

Published by the Penguin Group
27 Wrights Lane, London W8 5TZ, England
Viking Penguin Inc, 40 West 23rd Street, New York, New York 10010, U.S.A.
Penguin Books Australia Ltd, Ringwood, Victoria, Australia
Penguin Books Canada Ltd, 2801 John Street, Markham, Ontario, Canada L3R 1BA
Penguin Books (N.Z.) Ltd, 182-190 Wairu Road, Auckland 10, New Zealand

Penguin Books Ltd, Registered Offices: Harmondsworth, Middlesex, England

First published in 1989 by
Hamish Hamilton Children's Books

Copyright © 1985 Casterman, originally published in French under the title *Les Jours de l'Histoire: La Renaissance*

English translation copyright © Silver Burdett Press

Published by agreement with Casterman, Belgium

13 5 7 9 10 8 6 4 2

British Library cataloguing in Publication Data

Pierre, Michel
The Renaissance
1. European civilisation 1453–1517.
I. Title
940.2'1
ISBN 0-241-12762-9

Printed in Belgium

HAMISH HAMILTON HISTORY LIBRARY

THE RENAISSANCE

Michel Pierre
English translation by Nan Buranelli
Illustrations by Nathaële Vogel

HAMISH HAMILTON · LONDON

Preface

Within only a few decades, between the years 1450 and 1550, the history of the world was changed drastically. During that century, in which the modern world was born, Gutenberg perfected printing, Christopher Columbus discovered continents unknown to Europeans, Copernicus found that the earth revolved around the sun, Luther founded a new religion, the cannon and the harquebus ended the age of chivalry, and Leonardo da Vinci and Michelangelo created a new form of art. At the same time, most of the great European kingdoms were formed and national languages began to evolve. People started to call themselves French, Italian, Spanish, English, or German. Europeans planted their flags on the shores of every ocean. Artists, writers, philosophers, and humanists proclaimed that "nothing is more admirable than man." They rediscovered the heritage of Greece and Rome and proclaimed the *Renaissance*, the "Rebirth" of the spirit, of intelligence, of creativity, and of beauty.

Nevertheless, these same people who believed in a new kind of humanity held firmly to old prejudices. While they devoted themselves to mathematics and science, they

did not doubt the existence of werewolves, rainfalls of blood, and comets predicting death. And the century that saw the invention of surgery, the watch, and bank checks gave rise also to witch-hunts, wars of religion, the destruction of civilizations in America, and the first columms of chained black slaves.

In the villages of Europe, daily routines remained the same for millions of Europeans who were used to the unchanging rhythm of the seasons, limited by the dark lines of hedges or the neighboring forest, and subject to the authority of princes and the aristocracy. There the word *Renaissance* was unknown.

Johannes Gutenberg, Goldsmith of Mainz

During the Middle Ages, copyists were creating genuine masterpieces in the monasteries and in the "booksellers" workshops. They transcribed texts adorned by painted miniatures, and then painted illuminated designs alive with color onto very fine parchment. Covered by thick leather bindings, these manuscripts then remained in the libraries of abbeys or wealthy patrons, who alone were able to afford such lavish works.

Since they were rare and expensive, each one an original and reserved for a fortunate few, these books could not meet the demand of the many people who had learned to read and who were motivated by a real thirst for learning, for understanding, and for discovering the secrets of the universe. Students in the universities had to content themselves with inferior manuscripts, copied in haste, marred throughout by faults of transcription. Scholars, professors, and learned men of the time were forced to travel from town to town, from monastery to monastery, looking for works that sometimes existed only in small numbers.

Paper and Wood Engravings

By the end of the Middle Ages, however, progress was apparent in the reproduction of texts and illustrations. First came the invention of paper. Although paper had been perfected in China during the second century A.D., it was not produced in the West until centuries later. Paper is finer, whiter, and less expensive than parchment, which is obtained from tanned animal hides. It was produced in large quantities in water mills where hammers were activated to beat the scraps of flax and hemp needed for fabrication. At the same time, the technique of xylography, or wood engraving, was spreading. Texts and drawings, carved in blocks of wood, which were then soaked in ink, could be printed on a sheet of paper. But the procedure was imperfect, wood being a fragile base that rapidly wore out. Consequently, for each new text or drawing a new engraving had to be prepared.

Everywhere in Europe—Basel, Avignon, Holland—craftworkers were seeking another way to make impressions. In Mainz, a wealthy city on the banks of the Rhine, the banker Johann Fust was subsidizing the work of Peter Schöffer, a copyist and calligrapher, and of Johannes Gensfleisch zur Laden, also called Gutenberg. Gutenberg was a patrician and was extremely well educated. He had made a name for himself as a manufacturer of mirrors. But he achieved glory when he came up with the idea of making movable metal type that could be shifted and reused indefinitely to print pages that were then bound into books. Gutenberg's second creative idea was the use of a press, inspired by the wine presses of the Rhine winegrowers. With it, each sheet of paper could be firmly pressed on the "block" so that the type, arranged in lines and impregnated with thick ink, made of a mixture of lampblack, turpentine, and nut oil, imprinted itself on the paper.

The Forty-two Line Bible

In 1456 the Gutenberg workshop completed the printing of a three volume Bible of very high technical quality. This Bible was said to have forty-two lines per page; its type faithfully reproduced the gothic script being used then in Germany.

A year later, the *Mainz Psalter*, a work of Johann Fust and Peter Schöffer, was printed by the press. The name *Gutenberg* no longer appeared on the books; he had been expelled from the workshop by his colleagues. But posterity has rendered him justice by immortalizing him as the inventor of printing. Within a few years the new technique had spread all over Europe. Presses were working in Strasbourg, Paris, Antwerp, Lyons, and Madrid. Printers at the monastery of Subiaco in Rome invented Roman type. Others in Venice invented Italic type. By 1480, printers were established in dozens of cities. A considerable number of books were produced. Nearly 20 million titles, called incunabula ("the beginnings"), were printed between 1457 and 1500. By the end of the following century, the number of books was estimated at 200 million, not counting posters, brochures, and leaflets.

Within a few years, the price of the printed book, already only 33 percent of the price of the manuscript book, fell again. Books became accessible to the many who could read, and won this remark from an author in 1468: "God has given Christianity a gift which allows every pauper to acquire a book."

After many unsuccessful attempts, Schöffer and Gutenberg discovered that the best material for manufacturing movable type was a combination of lead, copper, and antimony.

Printing made possible the production of millions of minor works reflecting the popular culture. Peddlers went from town to town, from village to village, selling holy images, almanacs, chivalric romances, stories, comedies, songbooks, and books about the lives of the saints.

Revival of the Ancient Greeks and Romans

At the beginning of the sixteenth century, Felice de Fredis established himself in a fine property on the Esquiline Hill, not far from the Colosseum in Rome. Under the Roman Empire, more than a thousand years earlier, Nero's "house of gold," a fabulous palace adorned by dozens of marble statues, had stood on this hill.

Through the destructive action of time and humans, the columns and walls had crumbled, vegetation had grown over courtyards and rooms, and rank weeds and wild plants had dislodged mosaics and paintings. But reminders of the emperor's old residence remained, and Felice de Fredis, at the beginning of the year 1506, assembled a team of

workers to dig into the grounds and uncover the vestiges of marble that lay strewn around his gardens. At the end of the afternoon of January 13, the diggers struck a masonry vault with their picks. Feverishly they cleaned out the vegetation and removed the earth in their way. Nightfall, however, put an end to their search. Early the next morning a few sightseers gathered around the property owner and the painter Michelangelo, who had been summoned for the event. They watched as the workmen forced an opening in the vault at their feet. Their way lit only by the faintness of dawn, the diggers slipped into the hole. As their eyes adjusted to the semidarkness, they gradually made out the outline of a huge marble statue lying on the ground. It represented a man and two youths struggling with serpents entwining their arms, their legs, and their bodies. With infinite care the work was raised above ground. Michelangelo declared it a "miracle of art."

Scholars and artists rushed to admire the group, knowing, thanks to their knowledge of ancient texts, that it represented a scene described by Virgil in the second canto of the *Aeneid*. In this work the Latin poet tells of the death of Laocoon, a priest of Neptune, and of his two sons, who were bitten by reptiles risen from the waves. The pope himself came to look at the sculpture, and he bought it for six hundred pieces of gold. A month later the *Laocoon* left the Esquiline Hill for the Vatican museum, in a triumphal procession.

Fashionable Ruins

Following this extraordinary discovery, systematic excavations were undertaken all over Rome, and no European painter or sculptor could claim to be master of his art unless he had made the journey to the Eternal City.

Sculpted in the first century B.C. *by three artists from Rhodes, the* Laocoon, *was one of the most celebrated sculptures of antiquity. Many Romans, inspired by such discoveries, became entranced by the ancient history of their city. In 1544 one of them made a specialty of showing Rome to visiting foreigners and reading passages from Latin authors that described the monuments while the visitors regarded the ruins.*

Artists and writers liked to roam the Roman countryside to inspect ruins more or less buried in the ground. In this they were imitating Pope Pius II who, as early as 1450, had himself carried in a sedan chair to Alba, Tivoli, and Ostia to admire the remains of the antique splendor of Rome. In 1462 the supreme pontiff had even promulgated a decree forbidding the defacement of ancient monuments, to the regret of many inhabitants who, for centuries past, had been helping themselves to building materials from the ruins of ancient palaces, thermal baths, and amphitheaters. In imitation of the papacy, the Italian aristocracy collected statues, mosaics, and busts to enrich their collections of antiques. All over Europe, thanks to books, prints, and engravings, masterpieces from the ancient capital of the world enjoyed a true renaissance.

Early Italian Cities

Niccolo Machiavelli (1469–1527) lived and died in Florence. A writer and diplomat, he undertook to define the art of government in his treatise The Prince. *He dreamed of a united Italy.*

In the fifteenth and sixteenth centuries, Italy was the richest country in the West. The cities flourished, the countryside prospered, the ports were busy. Side by side with sheep raising and the traditional cultivation of olive trees, vines, and grains, new resources appeared, often oriental in origin. Thus Italian market gardeners experimented with planting artichokes, which became the favorite vegetable at aristocratic tables in the sixteenth century; while the cultivation of carrots, melons, and even rice became popular in the Venetian plains.

The white mulberry, originally from China, was grown in Tuscany and then in Lombardy. These trees in turn made possible the farming of silk worms. The silk worms' precious cocoons were boiled, then drained, to make thread for weaving sumptuous silks in Milan's workshops. Elsewhere, at Siena and Florence, wealth came instead from wool. In Venice, Genoa, and Naples, fortunes were born from maritime commerce. Pepper and cinnamon, arms and precious metals, pearls and leather, sugar and alum—that indispensable white stone used to fix dye in cloth—were unloaded on the docks of these seaports.

The World's Bankers

Because they brought in so much money, all these activities of commerce and production made Italian bankers the foremost in the world. They opened branches all over Europe. They lent money to kings and princes, frequented the fairs, and installed themselves in London, Antwerp, and Lyons. Florentine

florins and Venetian ducats became the most sought after currencies in the Western world.

At the same time, the aristocracy and wealthy merchants tried to make every large Italian city an independent state. As each city-state attempted to extend its authority over an ever broader territory, interminable conflicts arose. Unstable alliances pitted one city against the other. The Sforza family, whose most illustrious member between 1494 and 1500 was Ludovico the Moor, reigned over the Duchy of Milan. Ludovico was an intelligent and arrogant prince who liked to quip that he looked on "the pope as his chaplain, the emperor of Austria as his orderly, the doge of Venice as his chamberlain, and the king of France as his charger, that he made come and go at his pleasure."

Another dynasty, one of its most sinister examples being King Ferdinand I, controlled Naples. It was said that this king had two pastimes: hunting with the falcon, and collecting the embalmed bodies of his enemies clad in the clothes they were wearing on the day of their death.

The Italian towns were the most crowded in Europe. Six of them had more than fifty thousand inhabitants in the fifteenth century. Flamboyant wealth and extreme poverty went side by side. The sumptuous palaces of the great families dominated the poor quarters, where a population of craftworkers, laborers, and small-scale merchants huddled in houses without comfort or hygiene. The streets were disgustingly filthy. Rubbish and refuse, in which dogs and pigs scratched, were strewn over the ground. Over everything hung the stink of the dyeworks, the tanneries, and the slaughterhouses with their often-tainted meat. Exasperated by the conditions of their existence and by the smallness of their income, the lower classes, the populo minuto, sometimes revolted against the domination of the rich and powerful, the populo grasso. These riots against hunger and poverty usually ended in the massacre of the rebels, who were forced to continue in these miserable conditions until the next explosion of fury erupted.

Florence at the Time of the Medici

Federigo Orcellai is not the best-known Florentine of the Renaissance. Yet he has earned a snippet of glory in the city's history. In the fourteenth century, Orcellai brought back from the Orient a process that had been, until then, a jealously guarded secret. From Muslim craft workers, during a voyage in Egypt, he learned of a method of using lichens to yield a violet dye that had a most sumptuous effect. Florentine weavers and traders were quick to adopt the method, and the quality of their goods, which already was renowned throughout Europe, improved even more. From the Baltic ports to the cities of the Mediterranean, there was not a single market that did not sell the precious woolen cloth and the silks of Tuscany.

Empowered by the quality of its textile industry and by the richness of the Tuscan soil, Florence traded with the whole world. The city sent consuls to the Balearic Islands, to Egypt, to Persia, and to the borders of China. A great trading city, Florence was also the largest financial marketplace in Europe. There were more than thirty banks, the most powerful of which lent money to the sovereigns of the West, to the pope, and to all the Italian gentry. However, some of these princely clients were very bad payers. For example, King Edward III of England almost ruined Florence by eliminating a debt of 1.3 million florins with a single stroke of his pen.

The New Athens

The splendor of Florence was expressed in its cathedral, elegantly crowned by a dome and the first to be built since antiquity. It was designed by Filippo Brunelleschi, and built between 1445 and 1461. Great wealth was also displayed by the facades of the palaces owned by ranking families, who followed the advice of the architect Leon Alberti's proclamation that "the magnificence of a building should conform to the dignity of its owner." The city found glory too in the workshops of its artists, the most gifted and famous of the Renaissance; in the Tuscan language, which was assimilated by the whole of Italy; and in the schools where both Latin and Greek were taught.

Was there not a saying: "Athens has moved to Florence with its culture and customs, and Florence has absorbed it entirely?" Florence was an independent republic where any man could aspire to become an official functionary as long as he was a member of a trade association and up to date with the payment of his taxes. In reality, in the fifteenth century, power belonged to a few great families, among them the Medici, who dominated the others through violence, cunning, and corruption. Cosimo de' Medici, in 1434, began a dynasty that, in spite of revolts, assassinations, wars, and exile, ruled Tuscany until the eighteenth century. For three centuries the Medici illustrated to perfection this saying of Lorenzo, Cosimo's grandson: "In Florence one can hardly live well without being in power."

Lorenzo the Magnificent ruled the destiny of his city from 1469 to 1492. Having achieved power at the age of twenty-one, he wanted to be a poet as well as a ruler, and he prided himself on protecting all artists. Unfortunately, he neglected, more or less, the economic interests of his family.

Verrocchio's Studio

Usually apprentices were taken into an artist's studio at the age of about thirteen. Training lasted from six to eight years. The apprentice was fed, lodged, and clothed by his master.

Once the apprentice had demonstrated his talent or his devotion to work, he received a salary. After several years of training, he was ready to set up his own establishment.

At the end of the fifteenth century, the studio of the artist Andrea del Verrocchio was the most celebrated in Florence. People went there to learn to draw, to engrave, and to prepare colors and varnishes; and to study the laws of perspective and composition, the techniques of sculpture, and the arts of the goldsmith and the bronze-smith. Parents who placed their children there as apprentices knew the great reputation of the master, his passion for work, and his privileged relationship with Lorenzo de' Medici. Was he not the official curator of Lorenzo's collection of antiquities and the organizer of Lorenzo's festivals and tournaments?

In Verrocchio's studio, music and mathematics were also taught. The gossiping, idle rich liked to meet and spend time at the studio, treating it as their club.

The Decapitated Horse

The pictures were painted communally by Verrocchio and his assistants and apprentices, one of whom was Leonardo da Vinci. There is a story that at the time of the painting of a picture entitled *The Baptism of Christ*, the young Leonardo painted an angel of such perfection that Verrocchio decided he would never touch another brush in his life. The pupil, he said, had surpassed the master. But that is only a beautiful legend.

In 1480, Verrocchio left Florence for Venice to create the bronze statue of Bartolomeo Colleoni, a well-known general. In a short time he presented a plaster model of his work to the city authorities. He was about to begin work on the statue when he learned that another artist had received the same commission. Furious, he broke the horse's head off and left for Florence.

The Venetians informed Verrocchio that if he put a foot in their territory again, they would decapitate him as he had decapitated his plaster horse. He replied that there was no fear of his returning to Venice, since the Venetian senators did not have the same skill as artists in putting heads together. Eventually everything was straightened out. Verrocchio got his commission back and was even paid twice the sum agreed upon at the beginning.

It was to be his last work. While casting the bronze for the statue, he caught a cold and died of pulmonary congestion, at the age of fifty-six. While he lay on his deathbed, a priest presented him with a badly carved crucifix. The dying artist ordered him to remove it from his sight and to bring him one by his master, the sculptor Donatello. He wished, he said, to die as he had lived, surrounded by beautiful things.

Bartolomeo Colleoni was general in chief of the Venetian armies. He organized his command remarkably well, profiting from the rivalry between his different employers to build a handsome fortune for himself. At his death in 1475, at the age of seventy-five, he owned more than 200,000 ducats and many properties in Venice. The Venetian authorities ordered a statue in his memory, but they paid no attention to his will and sequestered his money and possessions.

Leonardo, Born in Vinci

The young Leonardo, a pupil of Verrocchio, received his first important commission in 1478. The Medici family asked him to draw the body of Bernardo Bardi, who had just been hanged for having conspired against Lorenzo the Magnificent. Scrupulously, Leonardo observed the expression of the face and the posture of the corpse swinging on the gibbet. And he sketched in the margin the condemned man's clothes: long black breeches, a hat, a satin doublet, and a cloak with a red and black velvet collar, lined with fox fur. With this most macabre commission began the prodigious career of a versatile genius, a true symbol of the Renaissance.

Leonardo was born in Vinci, a little Tuscan village, in 1452. He was the illegitimate son of Sir Piero, a notary, and Catarina, a peasant girl of the region. Very early in his life he came to love drawing, and he was apprenticed in Florence. For the rest of his life, as if to compensate for his illegitimate origins and for the classical education he never received, he studied literature and science and displayed an insatiable curiosity. He seemed to obtain all the learning of his time. His research led him to an interest in perspective, optics, mechanics, hydraulics, and anatomy (at the end of his life, he mentioned that he had dissected "more than thirty bodies of men and women of all ages").

Leonardo also wanted to be a poet, an astronomer, a mathematician, a musician, and an engineer. In 1482, wishing to leave Florence for the service of Ludovico the Moor, he wrote the prospective patron a long letter, boasting of his talents as a builder of war machines, a manufacturer of guns, and a sculptor. It is known, too, that he proposed to the sultan of Istanbul a plan to build a gigantic bridge over the Bosporus that would join Europe and Asia.

But for Leonardo, the first of the arts, and the most divine, was painting. He felt such an overwhelming need for perfection in this area that according to several witnesses, "he saw errors where others saw miracles," and "he seemed to tremble each time he started to paint."

His torment and self-doubt explain why he finished very few of the frescoes and canvases that he had been commissioned to do. But those that he did complete are counted among the supreme masterpieces of art; for example, *The Last Supper* (1497), *The Virgin of the Rocks* (1496), and the *Mona Lisa* (1506).

In 1516, after having lived and worked in Florence and Rome, Leonardo accepted the hospitality of Francis I of France. At the Chateau of Clos-Lucé, near Amboise, he died three years later still dreaming of new projects, such as the draining and improvement of the Sologne swamps.

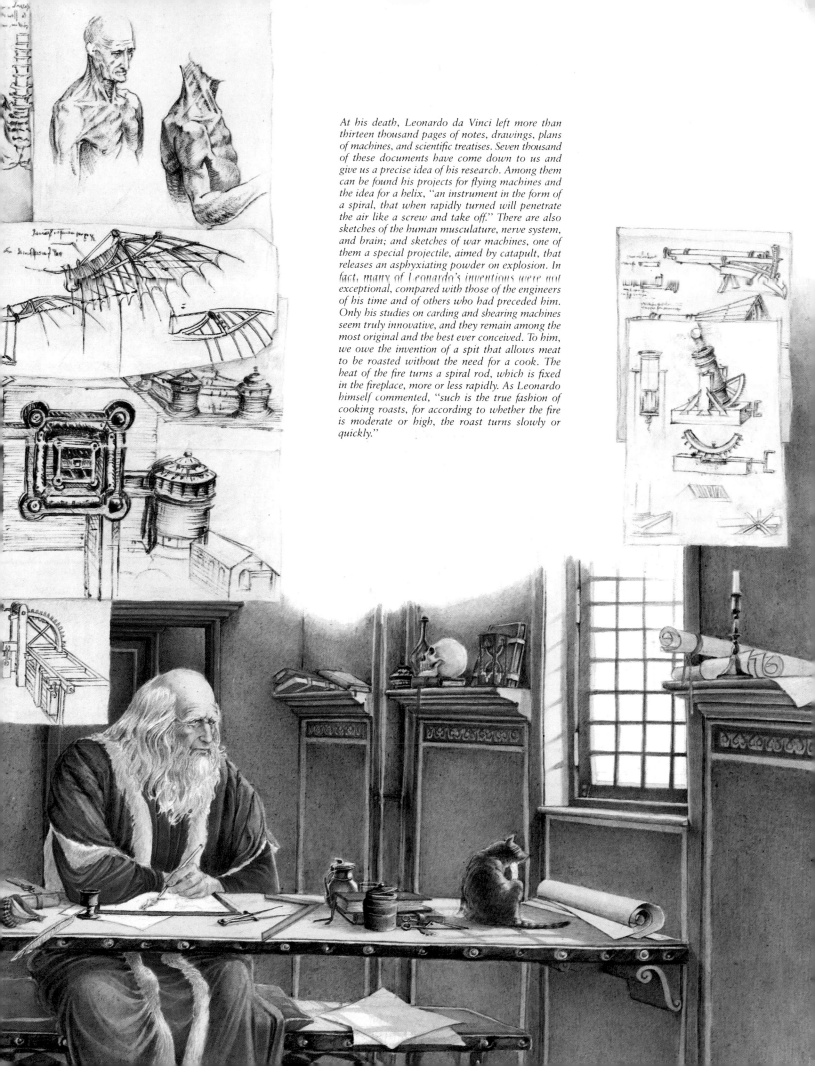

At his death, Leonardo da Vinci left more than thirteen thousand pages of notes, drawings, plans of machines, and scientific treatises. Seven thousand of these documents have come down to us and give us a precise idea of his research. Among them can be found his projects for flying machines and the idea for a helix, "*an instrument in the form of a spiral, that when rapidly turned will penetrate the air like a screw and take off.*" There are also sketches of the human musculature, nerve system, and brain; and sketches of war machines, one of them a special projectile, aimed by catapult, that releases an asphyxiating powder on explosion. In fact, many of Leonardo's inventions were not exceptional, compared with those of the engineers of his time and of others who had preceded him. Only his studies on carding and shearing machines seem truly innovative, and they remain among the most original and the best ever conceived. To him, we owe the invention of a spit that allows meat to be roasted without the need for a cook. The heat of the fire turns a spiral rod, which is fixed in the fireplace, more or less rapidly. As Leonardo himself commented, "*such is the true fashion of cooking roasts, for according to whether the fire is moderate or high, the roast turns slowly or quickly.*"

Rome, Capital of the Church

With their feasts, the pomp of their ceremonies, and their lavish building programs, the Renaissance popes were more like earthly princes than vicars of Christ. They often confused the interests of the Church with their own glory and personal fortunes; all this in the midst of a population ripe for insurrection. At the time of the election of Innocent VIII in 1484, the cardinal's votes were even sold to the highest bidder. Meanwhile, the crowd pillaged the wheat silos, the exchange shops, and the markets.

Among all the pontifical reigns, that of Alexander VI (1492–1503) was marked by the most despicable crimes. When he died, if we can believe a witness, "all Rome ran with extraordinary joy to see his body in St. Peter's, and could not feast their eyes enough on the death of a serpent who, with his

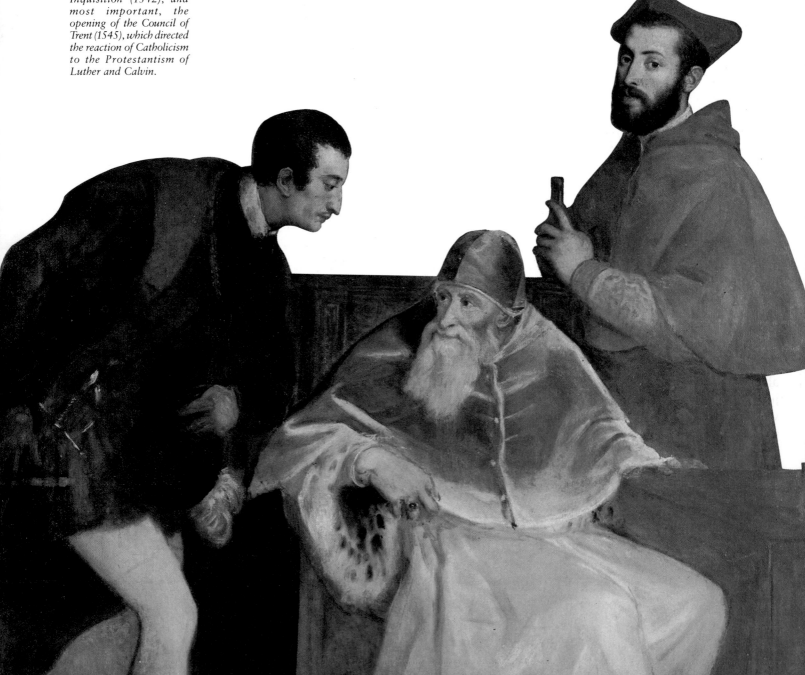

towering ambition, his pestilential perfidy, with every kind of terrible cruelty, of monstrous luxury and unbelievable avarice, even selling things sacred and profane without distinction, had infected the whole world." As for his successor, Julius II, according to Michelangelo, he preferred "the smell of powder to that of incense."

To celebrate his election, in 1513, Leo X organized one of the greatest festivals of the Renaissance. Amid a splendid procession, which traversed the streets of Rome for hours, the new pope had himself acclaimed by the Roman people. He was quick to follow to the letter the advice he had given his brother: "Let us enjoy the papacy since God has given it to us." In spite of their crimes and perfidies and their attachment to worldly goods, however, more than one Renaissance pope (there were twelve of them between 1450 and 1550) took the glory of Christianity and of Rome seriously. Many shared the pride of Sixtus IV, who was pope from 1471 to 1484. He boasted that he had received "a capital of mud and had left one made of bricks." Others, who came after him, left one of marble and stone, thanks to artists like Raphael and Michelangelo, who imprinted the works of their genius on the city.

The Christian West

Despite the popes with their ostentation and excesses and even their occasional violence, the Europeans remained profoundly Christian. Everyone believed in God and the devil, and everyone worried about his or her salvation, about the hellfire or eternal joy that divine judgment would bring. Every act of living was coordinated by the Church. It was the priest who baptized the people, married them, and administered the last sacraments to them. It was the church bell that announced the

The pope, head of the Church, successor to Saint Peter, lord of the pontifical states, and bishop of Rome, was elected in conclave by a college of cardinals. During the Renaissance the great majority of popes were Italian. It became traditional among the great Italian aristocratic families in general, and the Roman ones in particular, to do everything to have one of their own elected to the supreme post of Christianity.

great religious festivals, sounded the funeral knell, and gave the alarm. It was the Sunday mass that assembled the community on the Lord's Day. The Church also controlled teaching, from the modest "little schools" to the prestigious universities.

It is true that the priests, and especially the monks and the bishops, did not have a very good reputation. People realized their stupidity and made fun of their weaknesses for women and drink. But nobody would have been able to do without the religion that these men represented, in spite of their frailties and faults. Nevertheless, more and more Christians were calling for reform of certain abuses. They did not find an answer to their fears in the religion being presented to them.

21

Michelangelo

Like all the great artists of the Renaissance—Leonardo, Raphael, and so on—Michelangelo is known to us by his first name only. But in the registers of the little town of Caprese, near Arezzo in Tuscany, we can read that he was called Michelangelo, son of Ludovico Buonarroti Simoni, and that he was born on March 6, 1475.

Thirteen years later, as an adolescent, he entered the studio of the artist Ghirlandajo in Florence, as an apprentice. There he learned the basics of his art, showing a special talent for sculpture. He soon came to the attention of Lorenzo de' Medici when he copied beautifully an antique work that had been damaged over the centuries.

In 1496, at twenty-one years of age, Michelangelo fled from Tuscany, where famine and insecurity were rife, and went to Rome. There he created his first masterpiece, a *Pietà*, showing the Virgin Mary with the dead Christ on her lap. The beauty and perfection of the statue made him the premier sculptor of his time. This reputation was confirmed when he created the gigantic *David* (12 feet high!) that had been ordered by the Florentine authorities.

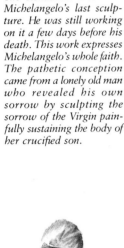

The Rondanini Pietà *was Michelangelo's last sculpture. He was still working on it a few days before his death. This work expresses Michelangelo's whole faith. The pathetic conception came from a lonely old man who revealed his own sorrow by sculpting the sorrow of the Virgin painfully sustaining the body of her crucified son.*

In the Service of the Popes

In 1512, Pope Julius II commissioned Michelangelo to decorate the ceiling of the Sistine Chapel. Michelangelo worked there for four years with fierce determination and astounding strength of will. He painted nine great scenes of the Creation, one of them movingly depicting God giving life to Adam as Adam emerged from the matrix of the clay. During this exhausting task, Michelangelo complained of his paintbrush, which dripped on his face; of his sore neck; and of his brain, which he claimed was damaged physically and mentally by the strain. The artist had also to face the pope's sharp anger, for the pontiff accused him of not finishing the chapel quickly enough and threatened to throw him off the scaffolding! *NICE GUY*

To the end of his days, Michelangelo worked for the papacy. As the supreme pontiffs succeeded each other, Michelangelo was always there, painting *The Last Judgment* on one of the walls of the Sistine Chapel, drawing plans for several buildings, proposing the design for the dome of St. Peter's Basilica. Sometimes, in discouragement, he would exclaim: "Paintings and sculpture, work and responsibility, have ruined my health, and it goes from bad to worse. It would have been better for me in my youth to have learned to make matches."

Michelangelo died in 1564 at the age of eighty-nine, still as tormented and despairing as ever, thinking perhaps of one of the dreams he had had as he roamed the marble quarries of Carrara in Tuscany: he had always wanted to carve a cliff overlooking the sea.

His Last Resting Place

The glory of Michelangelo was such that even his mortal remains were fought over. Some days after his death, he was buried in the Church of the Apostle Saints in the presence of the highest dignitaries of the Church and an enormous crowd. The pope expressed his intention to erect a magnificent tomb in the basilica of St. Peter's.

But Florence, too, demanded the honor of receiving the body of its most celebrated artist. Cosimo de' Medici had the corpse of Michelangelo stolen by merchants, who spirited it out of Rome, hidden in a bundle. A great catafalque was raised in a church in Florence to welcome him, and a funerary book was published, honors that were usually reserved for emperors. The body was then solemnly buried in the Church of St. Croce, not far from the ancient dwelling where the artist had worked during his lifetime. Nevertheless, his tomb still lacks the *Pietà*, which he hoped would adorn his final resting place.

Venice, the Sovereign City

The bells of the campanile in St. Mark's Square are sounding at full pitch. They announce the arrival of a fleet of galleys returning to Venice laden with incalculable riches. In the middle of the fifteenth century, Venetian ships regularly maintained the city's connections with the largest ports in the world.

From Constantinople and the Black Sea, ships brought back furs, salted fish, metals, alum, and silks. From Tunis they returned with gold and silver. In Flanders they loaded wool and cloth. In Beirut and Alexandria they found cotton and spices—for example, pepper, cinnamon, and ginger. The voyages were planned with great precision. The convoys left and returned on fixed dates. Venetian galleys, which could also navigate by sail, were swift and rarely were wrecked. They crossed the Mediterranean in four weeks; they joined Brugge (Belgium) with Venice in a month and a half.

But Venice was not just a maritime port of 150,000 inhabitants; it was also a capital of commerce linked to the Continent. Five great land routes led to France and Germany.

VENETIA.

Merchants from all over the Mediterranean, from the North Sea, from the Atlantic Ocean and from the Baltic Sea would meet each other in the streets and on the bridges crossing the many canals. The city merited the description that Philippe de Comines made of it in 1495: "It is the most glorious city I have ever seen, the one that grants the greatest honors to ambassadors and foreigners, the one that is governed with the greatest wisdom."

The Glassblowers of Murano

Famous for laces, woolen cloth, woodwork, and leather work, and the cutting of precious stones, Venice earned glory, too, from the works of its printers. By the end of the fifteenth century, they were producing almost half the titles coming off the presses. Moreover, the printer Aldus Manutius created the octavo format, which allowed the printing of books of small dimension.

The city was also famous for its soap factory and especially for its glassworks on the island of Murano. In 1463, Venetian glassworkers succeeded in producing "white glass," which allowed them, in the following decades, to make mirrors, eyeglasses, and telescopes as well as vases, plates, and decanters. The reputation of the Murano craftworkers was so widespread that a Muslim vizier (ruler) ordered four hundred lamps for mosques from them!

The wealth of Venice made it, just like Rome and Florence, one of the artistic capitals of the Renaissance. Artists such as Giovanni Bellini, Giorgione, and Titian knew how to imbue their canvases with an inimitable and luxurious light. They painted beautiful Venetian women who turned their hair "Venetian blond" by sitting for many hours on sunny terraces, wearing broad-brimmed crownless hats, with their hair soaked in quince juice mixed with privet sap.

The decline of Venice, however, was near. The Turkish conquests in the East and in the Balkans, and the great discoveries of the Spanish and Portuguese navigators were about to deal a fatal blow to Venetian development and wealth.

The doge was the leader of the Venetian Republic. Elected for life, his authority, his real power, depended on how he handled the different councils, the members of which were renewed each year.

The Crescent Versus the Cross

In the decades following the capture of Constantinople, the Ottoman Turks added to their empire. Syria, Palestine, Egypt, and North Africa were conquered. Suleiman the Magnificent, who reigned from 1520 to 1566, led ten military campaigns to Europe and three to Asia, at the head of 200,000 soldiers equipped with several hundred cannons. He seized Baghdad and Iraq in the East and invaded Hungary and Serbia in Europe before threatening Vienna.

After the prophet Mohammed died in 622, the followers of a new religion, called Islam, set out to conquer the world. In one century, Muslim warriors stormed over the Middle East, North Africa, Spain, and part of Asia. Christian Europe resisted as well as it could and tried during the Crusades to regain a foothold in the Holy Land, where the sacred places of the life and passion of Christ were situated. The Mediterranean region became the theater of a ruthless struggle between the faithful of both religions. During the Renaissance the struggle lost none of its harshness. In Spain, Christian knights aimed at *reconquista* ("reconquest") by concentrating on chasing the Muslims from the peninsula. At the other end of the Mediterranean, the Ottoman Turks, a new group of Muslim conquerors, were preparing to eliminate all Christian presence from the East. To succeed, they had to take Constantinople, capital of the Eastern Roman, or Byzantine, Empire since the fourth century.

The Death of an Emperor

In May 1453 the standards of Islam floated in front of a besieged Constantinople. The crescent moon, symbol of the Muslim religion, faced the cross of Christ's followers. Under the command of a young sultan, Mohammed II, twelve thousand soldiers and 350 ships of war blockaded the city, preventing any rescuing army from reaching it. Gigantic cannons blasted the walls, crumbling them into bits. These formidable weapons, the work of a Hungarian engineer, blew up the ramparts with their 1600 pound shot—the heaviest and most lethal ever made.

On the evening of May 28, Constantine IX, the last Eastern Roman emperor, said farewell to his relatives and councilors. He took communion for the last time in the Basilica of St. Sophia and spent the rest of the night galloping along the walls, encouraging the defenders for the last battle.

In the morning the Turkish armies threw themselves into the assault, crossed the ramparts, massacred the remaining defenders and a number of the inhabitants, and pillaged houses, shops, and monasteries. When the Muslim troops arrived in front of St. Sophia's hundreds of the faithful were still praying in the church behind the heavy bronze gates, which did not long resist the fury of the assailants. All morning sporadic fighting took place at several points in Constantinople. The roar of gunfire and the screams of combat were followed by the confused noises of a city in agony, the death rattle of the wounded, the cries of women, and the jeers of pillagers.

Searching the battlefield, the conquerors tried to find the emperor's body among the thousands of dead soldiers. When they finally found him he was recognized by his purple boots embroidered with an eagle, which only he had the right to wear.

Mohammed II then arrived in the city at the head of his escort. Sitting erect on his horse, he went straight to St. Sophia's, kneeled on the ground, gathered a handful of earth, and rubbed it over his turban as a sign of submission to Allah. He ordered that the church be made into a mosque but allowed the Christians to practice their faith and to keep other places of worship. His successors, however, were to have fewer scruples. They did everything they could to make Christianity virtually disappear from the new Islamic capital, which was later named Istanbul.

Mohammed II, conqueror of the thousand-year-old empire of Byzantium, had himself painted in a fifteenth-century picture, with a rose in his hand. Its perfume, no doubt, reminded him of the day his troops took the city, May 29, 1453, when the roses were in bloom.

The Atlantic Horizon

Equinoctial compass

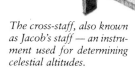

The cross-staff, also known as Jacob's staff — an instrument used for determining celestial altitudes.

The caravel, an astonishing ship to have conquered the seas, had its origins in the fishing vessel. This untried, unpretentious little boat was remarkably well fitted for navigation on the high seas. Its round hull and its prow and stern elevated into high foredecks offered good resistance to storms. The caravel often carried triangular lateen sails that allowed it to beat to windward.

In 1416, Henry, third son of John I, king of Portugal, withdrew from court and secluded himself at Sagres. This is the southwestern end of Europe, not far from Cape St. Vincent with its jagged cliffs thrust into the waves.

Fleeing the opulence of the court, the infante (prince), who had just turned twenty-two, began a task that kept him busy until his death, in 1460. Facing the sea, he organized a veritable research center devoted to the study of the stars, of geography, and of navigation. He surrounded himself with cartographers, astronomers, and dedicated navigators. He corresponded with everyone in Europe who was interested in pushing back the limits of the known world. In his library were heaped histories of travel, portolanos (maps of harbors), and books on navigation. Henry obstinately pursued one goal: he would give his country mastery over the maritime routes and thus take away from the Arabs and Venetians their monopoly of the spice trade.

As the years went by, Henry and his followers calculated, experimented, and set up projects in the greatest secrecy. All of them suspected that south of Africa there existed a passage into the Indian Ocean. They guessed, using simple logic and a few pieces of evidence, that by going around the Dark Continent it was possible to reach the shores of Asia, the ports of Cathay (China) and Cipango (Japan). The infante invested considerable sums to organize expeditions that resulted in the European discovery of the coasts of Río de Oro, Senegal, and Guinea.

In 1468, King John II resumed the work of Henry the Navigator. Methodically and with persistence, his ships pushed toward the south. Along the African coasts, *padroes*, stones claiming his sovereignty, were raised by the sailors who took possession of new territories in the name of the king of Portugal.

The equator was crossed in 1475, greatly frightening the sailors who could no longer recognize the familiar stars of the European skies. Seven years later, Diego Cão explored the mouth of the Congo River.

But the African continent seemed endless. All through the decades in which the exploration of its coasts was taking place, not a single strait, not a cape appeared that would allow access to the Indian Ocean. In 1487, John II decided to be done with this irritating puzzle. He ordered Bartholomeu Dias to follow the African coast "to the promontory where it ends." Two small caravels, supple and easy to handle, and sixty specially chosen sailors made up the expedition. Then began a trying voyage, during which the seamen encountered thick fog, heavy seas, and cold. After weighing anchor in a bay of southwestern Africa, they were caught in a tempest

and tossed about for sixteen days. When the wind calmed and the sky cleared, those aboard ship were stunned. The men, who had not seen the coastline for two weeks, now saw it, not to the east, as it had been since their departure, but to the west. Meanwhile, according to their compasses, the ships were headed due north. Without realizing it, the navigators had rounded the promontory they had set out to find. They christened it Cape of Torment. On their return, the king welcomed them enthusiastically and declared that "no-one has ever made Portugal a finer gift." He decided that the Cape of Torment would henceforth be called the Cape of Good Hope.

Ten years later, Vasco da Gama realized the great ambition of Henry the Navigator. During an expedition lasting almost two years, he circled around the tip of Africa, crossed the Indian Ocean, and reached the Indian coast. He returned to Lisbon, his holds loaded with pepper, amber, and gold worth sixty times the cost of the expedition, which had been enormous.

In a few years, because of the new commercial route opened by Vasco da Gama, the price of spices, which had created the wealth of Venice and the Arab merchants, was cut in half. Commerce moved from the Mediterranean toward the Atlantic ports. Lisbon became the richest city in Europe. The Portuguese established warehouses on all the African coasts along the route and in Asia. One of the smallest countries in Europe had built itself one of the greatest maritime empires. But already other ambitions were rising, among them those of Spain, which had just discovered a New World, thanks to Christopher Columbus.

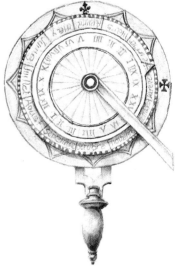

The astrolabe was a navigational instrument that plotted the position of the stars in relation to a given point. It was also often a superb work of art.

The work of the Portuguese navigators and cartographers was extraordinary. In a few decades they mapped 17,000 miles of the African coastline and 13,000 miles of the Asiatic coast. Each map was accompanied by indications of the latitudes, and the height of the stars and the tides.

Spain, Out to Conquer the World

In 1492, Christopher Columbus, a navigator born in Genoa, Italy, was convinced that he could reach the Indies by sailing due west. He succeeded in persuading the Spanish sovereigns, Ferdinand of Aragon and Isabella of Castile, to give him command of three ships, the title of admiral, and the viceroyalty of any islands or lands he might discover. They gave him letters for the Great Khan of China. On August 3, Columbus left the port of Palos in the bay of Cadiz, Spain.

First, Columbus called at the Canary Islands and then, after thirty-three days at sea and a relatively calm crossing, he discovered an island that the natives called Guanahani and that the Spanish christened San Salvador (one of the islands of the Bahamian archipelago). The admiral believed he was in the area of Japan and described his discovery as a veritable earthly paradise.

Back in Spain in March 1493, Christopher Columbus joined the court in Barcelona and exhibited Indians carrying parrots, rare plants, stuffed animals, and some gold. But the voyages that were then entrusted to him did not fulfill the hopes of the Spanish sovereigns. New lands were discovered, but the rewards in precious metals were minimal, and soon everything seemed to reveal that Columbus had not found the western routes to the Indies but instead a new continent, which, under the name of America, appeared in 1507 on a planisphere made at St.-Dié in the Vosges. The French cartographers were paying tribute to another navigator, Amerigo Vespucci, and not to Christopher Columbus, who had died some months earlier.

The First Voyage Around the World

After the voyages of Vasco da Gama and Christopher Columbus, the greatest maritime adventure of the Renaissance was undertaken by Ferdinand Magellan. At the head of five ships, this Portuguese navigator, in the service of Holy Roman Emperor Charles V (who was also the king of Spain), set sail in 1520 to carry out the first voyage around the world. He sailed due west, hugged the American coast, discovered the strait that bears his name, and penetrated the Pacific Ocean. But before he could complete his trip around the world, he died on April 27, 1521, having been attacked by the inhabitants of one of the Philippine Islands. His lieutenant, Juan Sebastián de Elcano, carried on and finished Magellan's task on September 4, 1522. The incredible voyage had lasted 1,080 days and covered 53,000 miles. Only a single ship, however, returned to port, and of the 275 sailors who had set out, only 28 survived.

In 1492, when he received the mission to conquer "the isles and continents of the said Atlantic sea, or any other," Christopher Columbus was forty-one years old, with a long experience of navigation behind him. Born in Genoa in 1451, he had roughed it on the Mediterranean as far as Asia Minor and on the Atlantic as far as Iceland. He had known battle at sea, had frequented many ports of the Western world, and had perhaps even dabbled in piracy.

Endowed with the intuitions of a genius and the flair of an extraordinary sailor, Columbus was a poor mathematician. In the end, he discovered America because he had wrongly estimated the real distance between Europe and Asia.

During his expeditions, Christopher Columbus wrote letters and reports about the voyage. We also have, from his own hand, a drawing of the three ships with which he discovered the New World. They were the Santa María, the square-sailed Niña, and the Pinta, which had lateen sails.

The Death of the Indians

Mexico was a huge city criss-crossed by large stone causeways and inhabited by lake dwellers. On June 30, 1520, after having occupied the town and massacred several hundred Aztec natives, the Spanish were driven out in a general revolt. In August 1521, Cortés retook the capital after fierce fighting. Spanish steel overcame the courage of the "eagle knights" and the "jaguar knights."

When the first Spanish colonists settled on the islands discovered by Christopher Columbus, they were soon disappointed, for they did not find the gold and the splendid riches they had dreamed of when leaving Europe. There were many who looked toward the American continent, toward terra firma, where, so it was said, fabulous cities paved with gold and silver were hidden away. Soldiers and men of the petty aristocracy looking for fame and fortune assembled expeditions, borrowing from bankers to equip themselves. In addition, the king of Spain authorized the conquests while reserving for himself a fifth of the spoils to come.

Under these conditions the conquistador, Hernando Cortés, at the head of six hundred soldiers, and with ten bronze cannons and sixteen horses, landed in Mexico on the shores of the Yucatan peninsula, in 1519. Before him stretched the Aztec Empire. The arrival of the Spanish coincided with ancient Indian prophecies announcing the return of gods who would come from the sea. This belief aided the progress of the conquerors, who also made sure to ally themselves with various peoples who were hostile to the Aztecs. The Spaniards, firearms, and horses terrorized an enemy who could only defend themselves with weapons of stone and wood. In just a few months, Cortés had seized the empire in spite of a general revolt in its capital, Tenochtitlán (Mexico City).

Ten years after Cortés, another conquistador, Francisco Pizarro, left a port on the

Pacific coast and arrived on the shores of the Inca Empire in Peru. With 187 soldiers and twenty-seven horses, he profited from a civil war that was ravaging the country and advanced deeper into the Inca territory. Pizarro set a trap for the Inca leader, Atahualpa, had him put to death, decimated the country's nobility, and pillaged and burned any resisting villages. All who opposed the domination of the Spanish conquerors (who were soon opposing each other) were exterminated. In 1571, when the last guerrilla war waged by the Incas had ceased, Peru, in despair, yielded to the strangers.

Invited to do so by the Spaniards, the Inca emperor entered the town of Cajamarca with six thousand unarmed warriors. Pizarro's soldiers massacred them, seized the emperor, and after obtaining a demanded ransom, put him to death. But even more than the massacres, it was the bad treatment meted out to the Indians and, above all, the diseases brought in by the Europeans that decimated the Indian populations. Millions died.

American Gold

Inca mask in gold.

One day, Christopher Columbus exclaimed: "Gold, gold, what an excellent thing it is! From it comes wealth, it is the mainspring of all human activities." This was an opinion shared by most Spaniards in the sixteenth century. The Mexico of the Aztecs and the Peru of the Incas provided the first cargoes of gold destined for Seville and Cadiz. Superb golden objects from the temples and palaces of America were melted into ingots before being loaded onto galleons that set sail for Europe.

This first trickle from the pillagers was followed by a real river of money after the exploitation of the Potosi mines in 1545 and the Zacatecas mines in 1548. Captive Indians, who died of cold and asphyxiation by the thousands, provided manual labor.

Slaves and Pirates

Stimulated by the trade in precious metals, the traffic between Spain and its American colonies expanded. Between the years 1500 and 1600, there were 11,500 ships that crossed the Atlantic, carrying provisions, munitions, animals, more than 300,000 emigrants, and 250,000 black slaves to the New World. On the sugar plantations the slaves replaced the Indians who had been destroyed by their conquerors. On the way back to Spain, the galleons, loaded with gold and silver, were attacked by pirates and buccaneers from France, England, and Holland.

Other, more peaceful means permitted the whole of Europe to profit from the Spanish riches. Emperor Charles V and his son, King Philip II, used gold and silver to pay their armies at war; to reimburse their creditors in Antwerp; and to buy wheat in France, textiles in Italy, and copper and iron in Germany. This outpouring of money upset the West's economy. It made the development of some regions possible, impoverished other areas and, in general, raised the price of products.

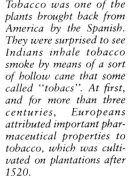

Tobacco was one of the plants brought back from America by the Spanish. They were surprised to see Indians inhale tobacco smoke by means of a sort of hollow cane that some called "tobacs". At first, and for more than three centuries, Europeans attributed important pharmaceutical properties to tobacco, which was cultivated on plantations after 1520.

European Bankers

In a little book published in Florence in the fifteenth century entitled *Advice on Trade*, a merchant speaks to a young man about how to go into business: "Your assistant, your protection, your honor, your profit, is money. This money must circulate and not lie sleeping in a coffer."

"If you have money," explains another trader, "do not sit back inactive. Do not keep it locked up in your house. For it is better to act, even if one does not profit, than to remain passive and still without profit."

During the Renaissance many people throughout Europe thought this way. They gave birth to capitalism and to the spread of commercial and financial activities. They supported the discovery of new maritime and land routes; established the bases of real industrial enterprises; and facilitated the development of metallurgy, mining research, naval construction, and printing. All this was made possible only by an outpouring of gold and silver that the Western world experienced after the discovery of America by Christopher Columbus.

Gold from Mexico and silver from Peru led to a tremendous growth at the exchanges. The discovery and exploitation of new silver-

bearing areas in Europe itself increased this expansion even more.

At the end of the fifteenth century and during the sixteenth, colossal fortunes were built. Dynasties of merchant bankers dominated all economic activity. Kings, popes, and princes often owed sums, considerable or not, to one great family of financiers or another and could not do without their services.

Jakob the Rich

The richest, most respected, most famous of these bourgeois dynasties was German. Founded in the fourteenth century, the house of Fugger of Augsburg, Bavaria, took admirable advantage of the town's location on the route linking northern Germany with Venice. To start with, trade in spices, silks, and cloth constituted the Fuggers' main activity. In 1473 a grandson, who was later named Jakob the Rich, took over direction of the business. Within a few years, thanks to the support of the aristocratic Hapsburgs to whom he had lent money, Jakob gained control of the Tyrolean and Hungarian silver mines. Later he was granted a monopoly on the sale of salt in Germany. Reimbursement came in 1519 when Charles of Hapsburg had himself elected Emperor Charles V. Of the 850,000 florins that the votes of the election cost him, 540,000 had come from the house of Fugger in Augsburg. The new emperor was not ungrateful to his bankers; he granted them new privileges, new properties, and new mines.

The Northern Ports

During the Renaissance the bankers' fortunes and the rapid strides made by commerce were also shared by the ports of the North Sea and the Baltic. The Hanseatic League and its prestigious cities of Lübeck and Hamburg launched more than a thousand ships. In the estuary of the Thames, London began the tremendous expansion that would make it the queen of the seas from the seventeenth century on. Antwerp became the principal port of the flourishing Low Countries, and in 1460 the first European stock exchange was founded there. At the beginning of the sixteenth century, one thousand foreign business houses had branches in Antwerp, linking this port on the Scheldt River with the whole world. In 1500 the city had more than 100,000 inhabitants and was profiting from the decline of its rival city, Brugge, a victim of the silting up of the gulf that joined it to the sea.

The gold currency of Florence, called florins, was used as a model for many European currencies. Each florin carried the lily of Florence on one side and the image of Saint John the Baptist on the other.

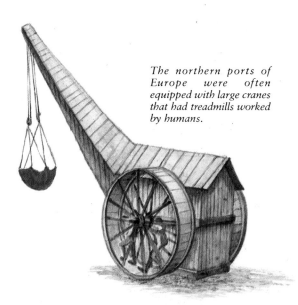

The northern ports of Europe were often equipped with large cranes that had treadmills worked by humans.

Dürer, the Traveler

Of all the paintings of the Renaissance, there is one very simple one that belongs among the greatest masterpieces. It does not show a mythological landscape or a sensual nude. It is not the portrait of a great personage nor is it of the Virgin and Child. It is simply a painting of a common tuft of grass. This watercolor in which every nuance of green is depicted, was painted in 1505 by Albrecht Dürer, one of the great geniuses of his time.

Dürer's talent astonished his contemporaries so much that Erasmus once wrote of him that he could reproduce with his brush even the human voice! "Dürer," Erasmus said, "succeeds in depicting what is indescribable: fire for example, rays of light, thunder, lightning, every sensation and every emotion, in brief the soul of humanity. And he can almost reproduce the very voices of those who model for him."

The Master of Nürnberg

Dürer was the son of a goldsmith in Nürnberg, Germany, where he was born in 1471. Instead of following in his father's footsteps, Dürer turned very early to the arts of drawing and engraving, and proved to be exceptionally gifted. In 1490, after years of apprenticeship

in a painter's studio in the town, he made his first journey to the Low Countries and to Colmar, Basel, and Strasbourg. He studied the works of the greatest artists of northern Europe before going to stay in Venice, between 1493 and 1495. During his travels he stopped often, drawing a landscape, exploring unknown towns, and meeting merchants and peddlers en route. He encountered the carriages and the fast coaches that carried the traders of Nürnberg to Italy in about ten days.

After his first stay in Venice, he returned to Nürnberg. By now he was a master of wood engraving and copper engraving, and his reputation was universal. In the workshop he ran, Dürer and his assistants produced stamps, paintings, objects wrought in gold, designs for sword sheaths, stained-glass windows, jewelry, and chalices and goblets.

When Dürer stayed in Venice for the second time, from 1505 to 1507, he was received like a great lord. He overcame the jealousy of the Venetian artists by proving his extraordinary virtuosity in the rendering of faces and hair. He was the greatest portraitist of his time, and the Venetian authorities asked him to make his residence in the city and become a citizen. But after a stay in Bologna and Mantua, Dürer turned back northward, toward Nürnberg, his only true home. Although he shared the anxieties of his fellow humans and was swayed by Luther's ideas, Dürer nevertheless remained profoundly Catholic. In 1520, the year of the coronation of Charles V, whom he met, he went off to the Low Countries. There he was entertained like a prince, and in Brussels he examined the Aztec treasures presented by Cortés to the emperor. "Never in my life," he declared, "have I seen things that gave me so much

pleasure. I am confounded by the subtle ingenuity of the inhabitants of these foreign lands." But Dürer's curiosity did not end there. In Brugge he bought a shield made of turtleshell. In Ghent he went to view a lion in the city's zoological park. Elsewhere he drew a walrus and tried to inspect a whale stranded on a beach.

When he died in 1528, he left behind more than a hundred paintings and almost a thousand drawings.

Albrecht Dürer's signature is one of the most characteristic of all those of the Renaissance painters. He finished the works that he felt most satisfied with by adding this large A on top of a smaller D.

War

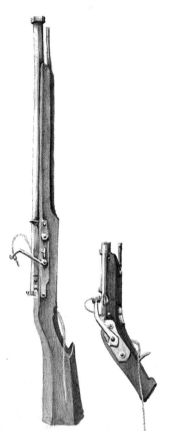

At the beginning of the sixteenth century, the Italian poet Ariosto wrote some lines railing against the cannon, the new king of battle:
"How is it, wicked and frightful invention, that you have found a place in the human heart?
Military glory is destroyed by you.
Through you the profession of arms has lost all honor.
By you, valor and courage are abolished."

The writer's anger clearly indicates the type of upheaval caused by the development of artillery and firearms. The perfecting of the cannon and the harquebus made conflict much more murderous than before. Strategy and the order of battle were profoundly changed. Cavalry charges and infantry assaults could now be disrupted by bullets and cannonballs.

Italy in Fire and Blood

During the Renaissance, Italy was the principal theater of European war. The country was prey first to the ambitions of the kings of France and then to those of Charles V. No province was spared by these wars, which lasted for sixty-five years, from 1494 to 1559. The wars were punctuated by occasional truces of long and short duration, some of which were respected and some not. Alliances were made and broken. Mercenary soldiers pillaged whole regions. The rules of war, which had been obeyed until then by the

When firearms were first used, at the end of the fifteenth century, certain war chiefs, hoping to preserve the traditional code of honor, had the hands of captured gunners and harquebusiers cut off.

condottieri, or leaders of mercenaries, no longer held. These army chiefs, responsible for engaging and paying their mercenaries, avoided excessive losses. They disdained encounters where the aim was to exterminate the enemy at any cost. And they were unable to understand the fighting spirit of the French troops. They condemned the *furia Francese*, the fury and folly of these soldiers who massacred their enemies.

As in every conflict, the civilians were the recognized prey of the hardened old-timers among the soldiers, who pillaged, burned, raped, and tortured. In 1527, Charles V ordered the taking of the holy city by his cavalry and foot soldiers to teach the papacy, which opposed him, a lesson. It was an occasion of massacre and destruction with few parallels in history. An officer who took part in the sack of Rome wrote in his memoirs some years later: "On May 6, we took Rome by assault, killed about six thousand men, pillaged the city, carried off whatever we found in the churches and anywhere else, and burned a good part of the city. When we went back to Rome in September, we pillaged again even more, and found some very great hidden treasure. We remained there in camp for another six months."

When the soldiers evacuated the city, they left behind them more than fifteen thousand victims—nearly a third of the population—massacred or decimated by hunger or epidemics.

The first big battle in which the power of artillery against the infantry was demonstrated took place in 1515 near the village of Marignano, not far from Milan. The seventy-two cannons of the king of France, Francis I, made drastic cuts in the opposing ranks, most of them Swiss mercenaries, more than eight thousand of whom were killed.

The Field of the Cloth of Gold

In the sixteenth century the sentiment of awareness of belonging to a national community, to a country, was developed. The sentiment was still a rare one for a majority of the different European populations, but it was gradually becoming more powerful. A Frenchman, Guillaume Budé, termed it "the genius of France"; Macchiavelli prayed for Italian unity; and, elsewhere, people regarded themselves as German, Spanish, Flemish, and so on.

Flying a flag with the arms of the king of England, the ship *Henry by the Grace of God* crossed the English Channel. It was a superb four-master with golden sails and with several guns showing their muzzles to port and starboard. On the bridge, planted solidly on his warrior legs, with hands on hips, Henry VIII, king of England, watched the coast of France draw near. In this spring of 1520, he was to meet King Francis I of France. Francis dreamed of enticing Henry into an alliance against Emperor Charles V, whose possessions (Flanders, Germany, Spain) nearly encircled France. But Henry VIII had already chosen his position. He would not help Francis I. The opportunity to weaken England's traditional enemy and get himself into the emperor's good graces was too good.

Yet Francis I had prepared things well. The first meeting took place on June 7, at Ardres, on the borders of French Picardy and the English enclave of Calais. An extraordinary village of canvas had been erected. In the center a huge tent 165 feet in circumference, entirely hung with gold brocade embroidered with *fleurs de lis* (the lilies of France), sheltered the king and his retinue. As far as the eye could see, hundreds of other tents, smaller than the king's but just as sumptuous, sparkled, painted with their coats of arms and mottoes.

The conversations between the two monarchs took place in a courtly atmosphere, punctuated by tournaments, banquets, and even an improvised jousting match—a struggle between Henry and Francis with their bare hands. A solemn mass was celebrated on June 23, after the signing of the treaty between the two realms. Three weeks later, Henry VIII would sign another treaty with Charles V, which annulled the most important terms made on the "field of the cloth of gold."

The Europe of the Great Monarchies

For nearly thirty years the three great princes of the Western world were to oppose each other in this way—ally themselves with each other, make war, swear peace, and make promises and never keep them. No game of alliances, no defeat, no victory could resolve the situation, although Francis I suffered a terrible defeat at Pavia. He was taken prisoner there in 1525 and was not released until the next year, after a humiliating treaty, which

Francis I, who reigned over France from 1515 to 1547, was a great lover of the hunt and of festivals and a protector of artists and writers. But above all he was one of the founders of a great state that he wished to unify and centralize.

A true Renaissance monarch in his splendor and his excesses, Henry VIII reigned from 1509 to 1547. A poet, a musician, and a patron of the arts, he spoke three languages. He made England into one of the great European monarchies and planted the roots of a reformed religion.

By the happy chance of his inheritance and of dynastic marriages, Charles V reigned from 1516 to 1556 over a huge empire that reached from the Danube to the Pacific and from Madrid to Antwerp. Two years before he died, he relinquished all his power and retired to a Spanish monastery.

he quickly repudiated once he had regained his freedom. In spite of the wealth of their kingdoms, the sovereigns could not terminate their wars because they were always short of money to pay their mercenaries and maintain the troops necessary for long campaigns. Charles V, the most powerful of the monarchs, possessed an empire on which the sun never set, stretching from Austria to Peru, from Spain to Flanders. But he had too many different adversaries to face, too many troubles inside his borders, to be able to mobilize his forces against France. He was obliged to struggle against the German princes in revolt and against the Turks, who were menacing Europe from the east and who controlled almost the whole Mediterranean. In spite of his efforts, his courage, and his intelligence, Charles V wore himself out at the task. His empire was too vast. It became impossible to govern, direct, or defend.

Henry VIII and Francis I had an easier task. Their kingdoms were all in one block, and they could impose their authority by being better administrators and by making sure of the docility of the nobility that they attracted to court.

Spectacle and Festival

Musical instruments were improved immensely and the types of instruments available diversified greatly. The human voice ceased to play an exclusive role in musical productions. The lute, the viola, and the violin became popular instruments. Some great composers also evolved during this period: a Frenchman, Josquin des Prés (1450-1521) wrote 22 masses, 129 motets, and 70 secular songs; an Italian, Giovanni Palestrina (1525-1594) composed 103 masses and more than 300 motets. When he died, he received the distinction of being buried in the basilica of St. Peter (Rome).

The splendor of the princely courts and the glory of the sovereigns could not exist without the decorations and pleasures of the festival. Balls, banquets, and receptions followed one another in an atmosphere of luxury. In a time when kings spent part of the year on the road visiting their domains and possessions or going off to the frontiers to make war, their passage through a town was a great festive occasion. For these "joyful entrances," painters and poets rivaled each other in artistic productions, banquets and balls were given for the king and his retinue, casks were broached for the people, and carillons and the chanting of high mass filled the air.

In 1520, Charles V made his way through Antwerp under four hundred two-tiered triumphal arches while young girls clad in light gauze and "almost naked," according to a chronicle of the time, portrayed allegorical scenes. Five years earlier, Francis I had been received in Lyons under a gigantic arch of triumph. The streets had been hung with tapestries and garlands of flowers. Open-air theaters presented tableaux vivants, or living pictures, among them the baptism of Clovis (a fifth-century king of the Franks who converted to Catholic Christianity) and the defense of the "Garden of France" (Touraine). It is even said that for the occasion, Leonardo da Vinci invented an animated lion with branches of lilies coming out of its mouth. Along the route taken by the king, each letter of his name was displayed. On eight columns 8 feet high were perched artistocratic young ladies, each symbolizing a virtue for each letter of the royal name. The *F* was acted by a girl holding a chalice and a host to signify the word *faith*. For the *R* of *reason*, another held scales for weighing wheat and silver. The letters were acted out in this way until the last one, the *S* of *sagesse* (meaning "wisdom or knowledge") was represented by a book held proudly above the heads of the enthusiastic crowd.

The Fork and the Napkin

During the Renaissance no festival was even possible without the pleasures of the table. Food was a sign of wealth; its abundance demonstrated the fortune of the host who had invited his guests to partake of good food and good wines. Ludovico the Moor was one such host. At a great banquet in his Milan palazzo, he offered his guests a menu worthy of Gargantua. Pies, marzipan cakes, and flat cakes baked on the hearth were served as a first course, followed by asparagus, roasted pigeons, calves' heads, and whole heifers. At the sound of trumpets, which announced each dish, the servants proffered capons, sausages, game, and chickens cooked in sugar. As a grand finale to this hearty celebration, the guests were offered ten kinds of tarts, preserved fruits, and jam. In comparison with what went on in the Middle Ages, this was gluttony.

Nevertheless, there was an effort to refine table manners. In the sixteenth century, each guest was given a napkin, a plate and a glass and sometimes a knife and a two-pronged

fork. These implements were beginning to be used, although it would be three centuries before the custom became general. Most often, fingers were used for eating, but, according to a manual of etiquette, people were advised to "pick up the meat with three fingers, and not to fill the mouth with overlarge morsels," and "to avoid putting meat in the mouth using two hands." As for the table napkin, precise instructions were given that it was not to be used "for wiping away sweat and blowing the nose."

The Hunt and the Ball

Just like their ancestors in the Middle Ages, the Renaissance aristocracy loved hunting, riding, and open-air life. Francis I was fond of staying in his castles that were close to game forests, such as Chambord and Fontainebleau. In the same way, Henry VIII, when he had depleted the deer park of his Windsor residence, would go off to hunt stags and roe deer in another of his forests or invite himself in a royal manner to stay with one of his favorites, whose hunting reservations he then royally attacked!

The princes also adored jousting; processions; chivalric festivals; and balls, where dancing took place to the sound of violins, trombones of Flemish origin, and kettledrums brought from the Orient. Gentlemen dressed in silk doublets and gentlewomen in luxurious gowns also took part in mummeries, masquerades during which masked women teased and seduced their galants who were disguised as Turks or Moors or who were dressed in antique styles.

Cookbooks were very popular. The first printing of a work devoted to cooking dates from 1475. The work of a papal librarian, it bears the fine title De Honesta Voluptate *(On Honest Pleasure). Fifteen years later a book in French appeared called* The Meat Book: How to Prepare All Kinds of Meat. *Meat was taken in a broad sense, since in these pages are found recipes for fixing storks, swans, and even slices of whale.*

The Beautiful and the Useful

Full of fine ideas and enamored of luxury, the princes and the rich noblemen of the Renaissance loved to surround themselves with furniture, ceramics, and ornaments of gold and silver, all of which displayed their wealth, their good taste, and their knowledge of ancient allegory.

The goldsmiths fashioned great numbers of objects: forks and knives of gold and silver, commemorative medallions, jewelry. They hammered and chiseled out masterpieces as their inspiration or the whims of their rich patrons dictated. On a little golden dragon, they would set gemstones, enamels, and pearls. They plated silver cups with fine decoration. They made little caskets of gold, silver, and ivory. Roman or Etruscan vases, found during excavations, were mounted on gilded stands, as were masks of jade brought back from America by the conquistadors. From Africa came ivory, which had many uses. A Florentine artist even made two spoons of ivory, one with a handle in the form of a bird, the other with its handle in the form of a jackal.

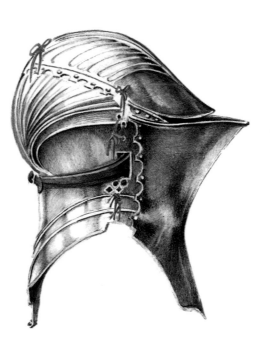

Ceramics and Wood

Italy, the country of the goldsmiths, was also celebrated for the art of faience, a kind of pottery covered with white tin-based enamel and decorated in color. In the fifteenth century, new colors were discovered for these decorations. To the green and violet already in use were added blue, brown, ochre, yellow, and orange. The town of Faenza in Romagna became so famous for making the ceramics that its name became the word *faience* in French and *Fayence* in German. In all their forms, faience plates, platters, glasses, cups, and dishes were objects intended for everyday use as well as for part of the decor. Dinner services often of more than a hundred pieces, were displayed and used. Sets of apothecary vases, the popularity of which was spreading throughout Europe, were also displayed and used.

Cabinetmakers worked to decorate and furnish the homes of the rich. Tables, sometimes covered in mosaics, rested on feet with carved whorls or motifs taken from antiquity. Beds were surrounded by twisted columns supporting a tester. Chairs, with their high backs, became more and more comfortable. Covered in leather, coffers lined with silk were carved, encrusted with gold, silver, and mother-of-pearl, or painted with mythological

This antique vase in hard stone, found during excavations, was restored and supplied with a foot, a handle, and a cover by Florentine goldsmiths, who added the Medici initials to their handiwork.

scenes. In the sixteenth century, the creation of furniture for display was started, including the making of *bonheurs du jour*, or desks, some of them with as many as eighty secret drawers to conceal documents and precious objects.

People of the Renaissance became more and more aware of the usefulness of measuring time, especially in the cities where the clocks of the belfries gave rhythm to the work periods. At the end of the sixteenth century, small, richly decorated clocks, for use in the homes of the wealthy, began to appear. The clocks were made by ingenious and original craftsmen, most of them from the German towns of Nürnberg, Augsburg, and Ulm. One of these clockmakers, Peter Henlein, invented in his Nürnberg workshop the first egg-shaped watches by using small springs to replace the system of weights. These first watches, called "eggs of Nürnberg," were worn around the neck on a chain of gold, in cases filled with perfumed essence.

Masters of Stone

Of all the Renaissance arts, architecture was considered the most sublime. To become an architect was the ultimate aim of many artists, from the most illustrious to the most humble. Leonardo, Michelangelo, and Raphael gladly would drop the paintbrush or the sculptor's chisel to draw plans, survey buildings, and make sketches of facades and designs for towers or domes of churches. Works of architecture were considered to be the most durable, the most spectacular, the most complete artistically, and the most clearly applicable to the great lessons of antiquity. The creation of a monumental work of architecture made use of every technique and every talent. A great construction site required the work of hundreds of quarryworkers, laborers, masons, and carpenters as well as glaziers, cabinet-makers, sculptors, and painters. All these artisans attained perfect mastery of their art and benefited from the technical advances and superior equipment they had at their disposal. Nothing seemed to be impossible for the architects. Did not one of them successfully move a church tower weighing 407 tons a distance of about 65 feet?

Throughout Europe, kings, popes, and great lords spent money lavishly so that they could leave in stone and marble evidence of

their power or their wealth. From the fifteenth century on, Italy was covered with building sites. Unlike the Middle Ages, however, the Renaissance period produced more civil architecture than religious architecture. More palaces and villas were built than churches, chapels, or cathedrals. The facades of the new buildings were organized in long horizontal lines pierced by windows and decorated with pilasters and columns. Beauty was expressed as geometry, equilibrium, and symmetry.

From Spain to Poland, from England to Hungary, architects took the Italians as their models, either copying them in a servile fashion or adapting the lessons the Italians had taught them to local traditions. Francis I, for example, brought builders and craftworkers to sites on the banks of the Loire and to the Île-de-France to "labor there in the fashion of Italy." All the great lords of the kingdom imitated their sovereign. Castles,

The castle of Chambord was finished in 1547, the year of the death of Francis I, who had taken part in its design.

houses, churches, fountains, and chapels triumphantly displayed the new style. In turn, the French masons and sculptors adapted and transformed, using their own imagination rather than merely copying plans and formulas from across the Alps. Dormer windows, for instance, and chimneypieces carried on a French tradition that resulted, in places like Chambord, in a dazzling display of imagination, fantasy, and virtuosity.

In the fifteenth century an anonymous artist drew the plan of this ideal city which is harmonious and balanced but almost cold in the interplay of its lines and perspectives.

The Farnese Palace in Rome was begun in 1514 according to plans of Sangallo. After 1546, it was built to plans of Michelangelo, who created many designs for the facade, using the great architectural ideas of the Italian Renaissance.

To Read, to Write, to Think

Born in Rotterdam in 1469, Erasmus, the "prince of humanists," who died in 1536, had a cultivated, tolerant mind. He did his best to maintain a Christian humanism that was soon swept away by the fury of the religious wars.

In 1487 the writer Pico della Mirandola, whose universal knowledge was celebrated throughout Europe, published a work entitled *The Dignity of Man*. In his preface he asserted, "Nothing is more admirable than man." This was a belief shared by thousands of scholars, writers, clerics, publishers, and princes everywhere in the Western world. These humanists knew each other, admired each other, and carried on an active correspondence between each other. They all shared the same ideal. They were enamored of life, of beauty, of knowledge. They brought to life again the writers of Greek and Roman antiquity and researched ancient manuscripts that were lost to the memory of humankind.

In this way, part of Cicero's writings were found, as well as some writings of Suetonius and Livy. Numerous Greek manuscripts, unknown until then, appeared in the West in the same way. According to the humanists, these works had to be read in their original languages. So the teaching of Latin and, in particular, of Greek and Hebrew was fostered. Rabelais had his character Gargantua write to his son Pantagruel: "I intend and desire that thou shouldst learn languages perfectly. First Greek, second Latin; and then Hebrew for the holy word."

The humanists loved to gather in small groups to discuss new ideas and the ancient civilizations. Certain princely courts in Italy, such as that of Ferrara, were frequented by poets, scholars, and artists. The Englishman Thomas More held receptions in his house at Chelsea in London, surrounded by his father and his three daughters.

The Triumph of National Languages

Along with the teaching of the dead languages, the use of national languages evolved. The Renaissance saw the definitive rise of the great European literatures. The Bible in German served as a unifying element for the different Germanic dialects, especially after the Reformation. In Italy the Tuscan language became the model to follow for all Italian writers. In England and Spain, works by authors writing in their native languages multiplied. In Portugal a humanist exclaimed: "May the Portuguese language flourish; talk, sing, and be heard. May it live. And wherever it may go, let it show that it is proud of itself." In France, Joachim du Bellay wrote *Defense and Illustration of the French Language*. In his preface to *La Franciade* (1572), an epic poem about the origins of the French monarchy, Ronsard recommended: "Use words that are purely French," and he advised that the national language be defended against "villains who consider inelegant all that has not been scraped from Latin and Italian." This movement was also written into daily life in 1539, when Francis I proclaimed the Edict of Villars-Cotterets, in which he ordered the deletion of Latin from the papers of judges and notaries and the use of French for all purposes. Of course, local dialects and patois would exist for centuries more, but French became the primary element unifying the kingdom.

The ideal of culture and the exigencies of learning encouraged the education of more and more children. But this movement touched mainly the nobility and the middle classes. Merchants, doctors, lawyers, and great lords were convinced that a man "who has read and retained what he has read is more capable of carrying out great enterprises."

In all the European countries, the number of inhabitants who knew how to read and write grew tremendously. At the end of the sixteenth century, it was estimated that 16 percent of the French people knew how to read and write, and in England the number reached 25 percent. This spread of knowledge was celebrated by Rabelais when he had Gargantua say: "The whole world is full of learned people, of able teachers and large libraries. In fact, I observe that the brigands of nowadays, the hangmen, the adventurers, and stableboys, are more donnish than the dons and preachers of my time."

Sickness and Death

In the sixteenth century, knowledge of the human body made considerable progress. Dissections, now tolerated by the Church, resulted in better understanding of the circulation of the blood, the position of the muscles, and the role of the viscera. Study of the fetus also led to the discovery of certain processes in the birth of a human being.

The man walking down the empty street is ringing a bell. Like a messenger of death, he is a few steps ahead of the cart heaped with bodies, their arms and legs dangling between the wooden guardrails. Occasionally, with a doleful screech the vehicle stops. Two gravediggers then move toward a corpse stretched out on the ground, lift if onto a stretcher, sometimes with the help of long tongs, and place it on top of the others, in a ghastly heap. Then the terrible retinue leaves the last suburb of the city and makes its way to a large field where a communal grave has been dug. The dead are emptied into it and covered with quicklime, before the convoy to the hereafter returns to a city in agony.

Since the beginning of the epidemic of the plague, hundreds of men, women, and children had been buried in this way. When a ditch was full, it was covered with earth, the place marked by a few stones, and a new hole dug. When the sickness struck, the town was isolated. No one went there; fairs and markets were no longer held. Some were able to flee to the country. Those who had to remain shut themselves up in their houses, burning balsamic herbs, such as rosemary, thyme, and lavender when they could. In the heavily scented rooms, each person watched the others for signs of the first symptoms, which were boils, or great swellings, in the groin or the armpit, almost irreversible signs of coma and death. Sometimes, fear of the sickness became madness. Faced with the

unbearable wait, according to a chronicle of the time, some threw themselves into a well or the river, or "banged their heads against the wall until their brains came out." In the hospitals were piled the sick, with doctors and nuns attempting to care for them. At the same time, priests went around to take the last sacraments to the dying. To die in the hospital meant that there was at least hope of being buried in a real coffin or in a shroud.

The Black Death

The plague appeared in the West in the middle of the fourteenth century, killing off one European in three. In the course of the following centuries, it continued its ravages. In 1484 more than fifty thousand victims were counted in Milan, and nearly as many in Florence, in Bologna, and in Rome in the weeks that followed. In 1520, four thousand people died in Avignon, seven thousand in Limoges in 1547, sixty thousand in Lyons in 1560, forty thousand in Paris in 1566, fourteen thousand in Bordeaux in 1585. In Germany, in England, and in Flanders the dead could also be counted in tens of thousands all through the sixteenth century.

Medicine remained helpless in the face of such a scourge, even though people were beginning to guess that crowding the inhabitants of the towns into unsanitary areas was favorable to the propagation of a sickness not yet known to be carried by the fleas on rats.

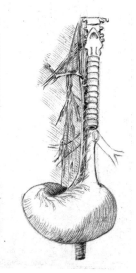

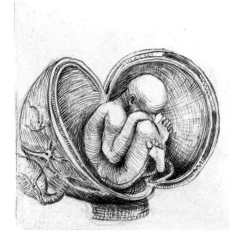

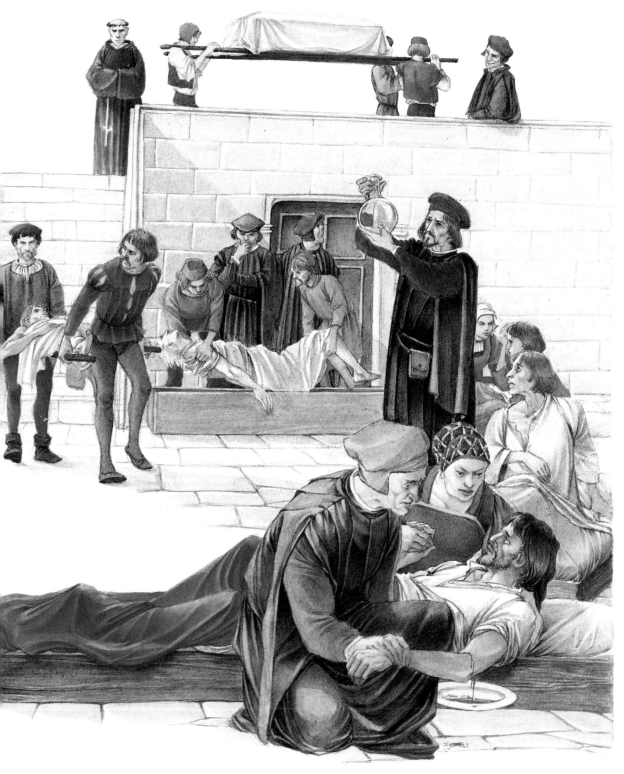

During the Renaissance a doctor was a learned personage who spoke Latin and knew the ancient texts—but who could not bear to see blood flow. He left the tasks of bleeding and the treatment of wounds and amputations to those who were used to handling sharp instruments—that is, the barbers. From their ranks gradually emerged the surgeons, proud of their skill and of the progress they were making in the name of science. One such example was Ambroise Paré, who knew not a word of Latin but could extract the bullet from a harquebus wound as no one else could.

Devils, Witches, and Sorcerers

When the plague ran from city to city, from one province to another, destroying the population of a village and annihilating entire neighborhoods, no one could understand the implacable violence of such a curse. Everyone, from the peasant to the priest, from the doctor to the craftworker, was convinced that the sickness came either from divine anger or the wickedness of Satan. Confronted with the epidemic, they looked for people to blame. They tracked down all those who were different, who were on the road, the strangers, the disreputable, the non-Christians. Everywhere, Jews were massacred, beggars put in prison, and prostitutes arrested. Sorcerers and witches were also under suspicion. It was suggested that they propagated the plague "by preparing deadly compounds made of spiders, juice from boils, and toads' spittle and mixing it with pitch or animal fat so that the poison would stick to the seats in the chapels and cathedrals."

The Broomstick and the Sabbath

Subject to nature but ignorant of her laws, the men and women of the Renaissance, like their ancestors of the Middle Ages, lived surrounded by supernatural signs. According to the people, demons were wandering around their cottages, causing hailstorms, fires, floods, droughts, and sickness. Everyone believed in the stone that could make you invisible, and everyone believed in wonders such as human beings who turned into werewolves and ate children. Many asserted that the future could be foretold by someone who had swallowed the still-beating heart of a dove.

A dead cow, a sick sheep, a drowned child, a fire in the barn, a black cat crossing the road, a man becoming impotent, a woman dying in childbirth—all were signs proving Satan's interference through his earthly followers, the sorcerers and particularly the witches. Indeed, it was believed that woman was driven by seven different motives into frequenting the devil. These were first her credulity, then her curiosity, her more impressionable nature, her greater malevolence, her desire for revenge, her ease of despair, and finally, her gossipy nature. Some women were believed to fly from their houses astride a broomstick on the way to a witches' Sabbath, where they would meet the black goat, under whose features was hidden the master of hell. During those nights of orgy, held by all the witches of a region, horrible doings were decided on; poison recipes and

magic philters were exchanged. In all those doings, woman was often revealed to be, as a proverb of the sixteenth century put it, "an imperfect beast, without faith, without law, without fear, without constancy."

To discover which men and women in a population were in league with the devil, learned books were written. Those books explained how to outwit suspects, how to arrest them and interrogate them (with or without torture), how to condemn them and send them to their death. In the atmosphere engendered by such beliefs, anyone could be guilty. The least gesture a little bit out of the ordinary, just one slightly bizarre word, the tiniest jealousy of a neighbor, even the minimal use of a plant-based medication could bring on accusations of witchcraft. And rare were those men and women, especially women, who escaped torture, once accused, and who did not confess everything the judges wished to hear. Then the logs of the woodpile were ignited.

It was in the year 1275 at Toulouse that the first witch was burned. But it was in the sixteenth and seventeenth centuries that the witch trials and executions multiplied. Mainly in France, Germany, and England, several thousand people perished in the flames.

A New Religion

Martin Luther was born in Eisleben in Saxony in 1483 into a lower middle-class family of peasant origin. In 1505 he dedicated himself to the monastic ideal. He became an Augustinian monk, was ordained a priest in 1507, and ranked as a doctor of theology. He distanced himself from the Church of Rome before breaking off relations with it entirely. Excommunicated and rejected, he was given refuge in the castle of the elector of Saxony, where he translated the Bible into German and established the basis for a new faith. He later opposed the peasants who revolted in the name of his own theories. In 1546 he died, affirming his absolute faith in Christ.

The men and women of the Renaissance loved life just as much as they feared death. They were tormented by fears of a brutal end that would take them before divine justice without the chance to receive the last sacraments, which would have allowed them to escape an eternity of punishment.

For many of those who lived in this fear, there was little reason for hope. The clergy seemed corrupt, and the pope and the bishops were great lords whose main interests were pleasure and earthly riches. Now, thanks to printing and to the distribution of the Bible and the holy texts, more and more Christians had access to the teachings of the Gospels. There they found more cause for reflection and hope than in the sermons of their priests, who were frequently made fun of and despised and sometimes even detested.

The only response the Church seemed able to make to ensure the salvation of souls was the practice of selling indulgences. In exchange for rather considerable sums of money or for pilgrimages accompanied by charitable donations, the Church allowed a glimpse of the hope of paradise and a reduction in the number of years to be spent in purgatory, either for the donor or for his or her dead. The papacy, needing money, especially for building the Basilica of St. Peter in Rome,

encouraged this trade. Thus, preachers swarmed over Germany, wooden bowls in hand, asserting that "as soon as silver tinkles in the bowl, the soul will be released from the sufferings of purgatory."

The Monk Who Rebelled

This time it was too much. Martin Luther, an Augustinian monk in Wittenberg, Germany, and a doctor of theology, protested. On October 31, 1517, he made public ninety-five "theses" and undertook to defend them against all who cared to argue the issues with him. This was just current practice, but by attacking indulgences and thereby challenging certain pontifical decisions, Luther brought down on his head the wrath of Rome. In 1520 in three great statements, he deepened his criticisms and made his ideas more explicit. He asserted that the pope, like all Christians, was subject to the authority of the biblical texts and that nothing but the holy scripture counted—not tradition, not the rulings of the councils, not even the papal edicts them-

selves. Luther's ideas seduced a number of Christians. Luther was convincing when he stated that only faith saves the Christian from damnation, that one must believe in the grace that God grants or refuses according to his will, which is beyond the comprehension of humans.

Little by little the rupture between Luther and the pope became absolute. Luther was excommunicated in 1521, and Emperor Charles V, who supported the pope, banned Luther from the Holy Roman Empire. This terrible act meant that anyone could put Luther to death without fear of pursuit; that everyone was forbidden to print, sell, buy, or keep his books; and that priests could not discuss or even mention his ideas in their sermons.

However, there were certain German princes who upheld Luther's ideas. Rejecting in their turn the pope's authority, they were really hoping to seize the Church's property. Charles V, who at first had been obliged to allow all princes the freedom to choose their religion and to impose it on their subjects, now tried

Born in Noyon in 1509, John Calvin, a Frenchman, carried on Luther's work. He insisted on the power and absolute authority of God and dreamed of a Christian state where all the virtues would be practiced. Living in Geneva from 1541 to 1564, he tried to make the city a model for the new way of life and thought, from which libertines and papists were banished.

From Geneva, Calvinism spread across Europe—into France, the Low Countries, and the British Isles—and became the most important of the churches born of the Reformation.

to reverse his decision. The princes who backed Luther "protested" and united their forces. It was war. In the end the emperor had to accept the division of Germany between Catholics and Protestants.

In his writings in 1520, Luther not only attacked the pope's authority but also denounced the sacraments, keeping only Baptism and the Eucharist. He opposed the celibacy of the clergy and monastic vows. Leo X then promulgated a papal bull condemning Luther, who marked his complete rupture with papal authority by burning the papal text in the square of Wittenberg, Germany, on June 15, 1520.

Massacres in Christ's Name

When Luther was excommunicated on January 3, 1521, Erasmus wrote: "I am afraid that one day this affair will end in carnage." The Rotterdam humanist was not mistaken. The struggle that was beginning between Catholics and Protestants would go on for almost two centuries. The religious civil war that tore the West apart brought with it massacres, ruin, and misery.

The victims numbered in the tens of thousands in a stream of atrocities in which Christian virtues were not apparent. In Germany the religious unrest was sparked by a peasant uprising against the nobility. Many of the rebels carried out their actions in the name of the reformed religion and of divine justice. They attacked castles, monasteries, and convents; besieged the cities; and killed the priests and aristocrats who had been seized. An army of nobles and mercenaries was formed to confront the insurrection. This reaction was a measure of the fear felt by the nobility. Their well-equipped armies annihilated the peasant forces. Their prisoners were systematically executed. One executioner even boasted of having cut off twelve thousand heads! During the last battle, in Alsace, the Duke of Lorraine was said to have ordered that the twenty thousand prisoners taken by his men-at-arms and knights have their throats cut. Many people believed that this was actually done, but the number alone makes the story unbelievable.

In France the era of great violence really began after the Amboise Conspiracy in 1560, when Protestants tried to kidnap the young king, Francis II. The reaction of the Catholics was ruthless. Regnier de la Planche has left a horrifying testimony on the subject: "So, several days a month were employed in cutting off heads, or in hanging or drowning. And indeed, on the River Loire could be found sometimes six, eight, ten, twelve or fifteen bodies attached to poles, still with their boots on, so that such a piteous sight was never seen. The streets of Amboise were running with blood and carpeted everywhere with dead bodies, so that one could not endure the stink and infection of the city."

In Spain, King Philip II, successor to Emperor Charles V, eliminated Protestants from his kingdom by ordering great autos-da-fé, enormous public executions or bonfires where all who upheld the reformed religion died in the flames, were decapitated, had their throats cut, or were disemboweled.

In England it was the Catholics, priests mostly, who died in the flames, were beheaded, had their throats cut, or were disemboweled. In the Low Countries, churches were ransacked and monks put to death. Some people were buried up to their necks, their heads being used as targets by bowlers.

Often, religion was only a pretext to justify the pleasure of killing and the lust for pillage. Religion allowed the chiefs of bands of the petty nobility to live on extortion and violence, as did those described by the Gascon poet Guillaume Ader: "Neither force nor cunning will make these people carry a pen at their girdles. They prefer a nice little dagger to put at your throat as they seize you by the neck."

A New Universe

He was called Nicolaus Copernicus and was born in Torun in the north of Poland in 1473. He did not perfect printing, like Gutenberg, nor discover a new continent, like Christopher Columbus, nor did he turn Christianity on its head, like Luther. Perhaps, though, Copernicus did more. He changed the position of the earth in the universe.

The Student of Kraków

In 1491, Nicolaus Copernicus, a member of a rich merchant family, was admitted into Jagellon University of Kraków, Poland. At the time, this university was the only one in all Europe to have two chairs of astronomy. It enjoyed a universal reputation for the teaching of mathematics. There the young man learned the movements of the stars. Relying on certain passages in the Bible and on the writings of the Greek authors Aristotle and Ptolemy, the university taught that the earth was the center of the universe. Around the earth turned the sun, a diaphanous, burning mass, accompanied on its way by the procession of the planets. As humankind ruled over the land, so did the earth, motionless and serene, reign over the cosmos. And even if these statements suffered from many contradictions and anomalies, no one was going to cast any doubt on the witness of the Holy Scriptures and the texts of the ancient masters. Thanks to the support of an uncle, the bishop of Warmia in Poland, Nicolaus Copernicus planned an ecclesiastical career and remained passionately interested in the study of the universe. After four years at Kraków, he went to Bologna in Italy, where he perfected his learning of astronomy.

Through mathematical analysis, geometry, and observation of the sky, he acquired the glimmerings of a new explanation of the movement of the stars. After Bologna, Copernicus made a stay in Rome, returned to Poland, and then went back to Italy. There, in Padua, he entered the faculties of law and medicine. In Ferraro he was made a doctor of canon law (May 1503). Now, endowed with a solid background of scientific knowledge acquired during his student years, Copernicus, who had become a canon at Frombork in his native Poland, could devote himself to his research. He had an observatory built, and he remained in this town until his death.

For thirty-six years he worked and observed. He calculated the distances of the different planets from the sun and gave reasons why the moon is a satellite of the earth. He explained the changing of the seasons and the inequality of days and nights. He gave himself up entirely to preparing his book *De*

We know the face of Nicolaus Copernicus, thanks to a self-portrait now lost to us but a copy of which was made in the sixteenth century and is preserved in the town hall of Torun, the sage's native town.

NICOLAVS COPERNICVS.

Revolutionibus Orbium Coelestium (Concerning the Revolution of the Planets). Copernicus said that "the center of the earth is not the center of the universe." He also believed that the earth was a planet like the others, no more important or different than they, and that it revolved around the sun. "What seems to us to be the movement of the sun is due not to its displacement but to a displacement of the earth, in the course of which we revolve around the sun like any other planet."

The work was not printed until 1453, by a printer in Nürnberg. Aware of having overturned the accepted order of the universe, Copernicus was careful to dedicate his book to Pope Paul III, and he presented his system as merely a hypothesis. The pope accepted the book, but much later some church authorities reacted violently and condemned such writings, which questioned certain statements in the Bible. More than a century was to pass before the theories of Copernicus were accepted definitively.

Written in the script of the time, Copernicus's manuscript De Revolutionibus Orbium Coelestium *is illustrated by many drawings and diagrams showing the orbit of the earth around the sun and the position of the different planets (Mars, Venus, Mercury, Saturn, and so on).*

A French Village in 1550

As he does every Sunday during mass, the priest has just intoned: *A peste, fame et bello, libera nos, Domine.* Among the faithful who repeat his words, not one understands Latin, but all know that the priest, as priests have done for centuries, is asking God to deliver them "from the plague, from hunger and war." Through the long years, these three reapers of death keep watch on the outskirts of the village, and it is not rare for them to appear together and sow destruction.

In the church, in front, on the seat reserved for him, sits the *seigneur*, the lord of the manor. Ruthless in matters of money, jealous of his rights and privileges, owner of broad acres, he arbitrates disputes between the villagers and does not disdain to mingle with them during certain festivals. But he is detested when he hunts with his friends, crossing the fields and laying waste to the villagers' crops.

Not far from the seigneur and his family are some farmers who own their land and succeed in making some money by selling a part of their harvest at the market. Some of them can read a little, write a little, and above all, count. There is also the innkeeper, the wheelwright, the blacksmith, a mason who is also a carpenter, a maker of wooden shoes, all of them peasants but also owners of some plots of ground. But the greatest number of the village's inhabitants are humble people—laborers, field hands, and so on. They work in the fields belonging to others and cultivate some patches of land for themselves. In their one-room, mud-walled cottages, they are often heads of large families. Since they depend so much on others for their survival, they are the first to be touched by bad crops, famine, and crises.

The Boundaries of the Village

In the France of the good king Francis I, there were about thirty thousand villages. In them, lived nearly 85 percent of the 18 million

In the sixteenth century, the peasants profited from the general economic improvement. Market gardens were developed around the villages, the fairs were well attended, and the demand for meat and cereals increased markedly. Life was quite comfortable in some regions prior to the difficult times at the end of the century.

inhabitants of the kingdom. There were many differences between the regions: great plains in the north and in the Paris basin, woods in Brittany and Normandy, heaths and moors in Provence, fine fields and vineyards in Aquitaine. Everywhere, grain was cultivated— wheat, rye, barley, or buckwheat—according to the nature of the soil. Vines grew almost everywhere, limited only by the climate. Everywhere, too, there were forests, but especially there were heaths, marshes, and brush.

The village and the lands around it made up the area that was familiar to the villagers. They seldom left it, marrying there, living and dying in the shadow of the belfry. Their only links with the outside world were the king's agents or the peddlers who came to hawk bright-colored ribbons, sachets of spices, saw blades, pious images, devotional manuals, and almanacs. It was the agents and peddlers who brought news of happenings in the world, who informed the villagers of somber or agreeable news.

Sometimes, when life was too hard, the overlords too greedy, taxes too heavy, or injustice too great, a revolt would explode. It was a despairing display of violence by people who felt they had nothing left to lose. Repression after the uprising was always ferocious. The trees would be covered with hanged bodies, the fields strewn with corpses, and cottages ablaze. When peace returned, it was the peace of death.

In the thousands of villages in France, who among all these millions of people who could neither read nor write had ever heard the word *Renaissance*?

Renaissance Painting

During the Renaissance the art of painting was profoundly altered. Everything was turned around—the techniques, the materials, the subjects of inspiration, and also the role of the artist in society.

Painting the Truth

In the Middle Ages the art of Italian painters was mainly religious in inspiration. Christ, the Virgin, and the saints had long impassive faces topped by gilded halos. They were placed one against the other without regard for perspective and according to assumed rules inherited from the art of Byzantine mosaics and icons.

From the fourteenth century on, some artists began slowly to break away from this style, abandon these conventions, and open their eyes to what they saw around them. They were interested in nature, in man and woman, in their bodies, in the true character of their faces, even if they were ugly or deformed. In the antique statues that were being brought out of the ruins, they discovered the beauty of the human form, the emotive power of the nude. They drew fresh inspiration from texts of Greek and Roman authors, and they multiplied allegorical and mythological themes. The passion for antiquity became such that a painter like Masaccio would sign one of his works with his name in Greek characters. By opening their eyes to the nature surrounding them, by studying the people of their own time, and by applying the lessons of the past, the painters of the Renaissance expanded the limits of their art. Through the interplay of colors, lighting, and geometric lines, they created the illusion of space and invented perspective.

Oil and Canvas

Until the fifteenth century, painters used the technique of fresco a great deal. First they spread a coating of plaster with a chalk and sand base on a wall. On this fresh coating (called *fresco* in Italian, a word since adopted into English), they drew their outlines and applied their colors, working quickly, since the plaster dried rapidly. This method made paintings last a very long time. But much preparation was needed along with great rapidity of execution, and it was impossible to retouch the work.

Painting in oil, first introduced in Flanders, solved this problem. Henceforth the painter mixed his colors with oil (often linseed or nut

During the Renaissance the art of the portrait reached the height of perfection. By dwelling on the psychological truth of their models and successfully rendering the luxury of the cloths, the velvets and the furs, painters produced genuine masterpieces, such as this portrait of Baldassare Castiglione by Raphael (The Louvre).

Sacred and Profane Love *by Titian, the most celebrated Venetian artist of his time, marvelously expresses Renaissance painting: the taste for light, the pleasure taken in painting bodies, the symbolism of actions and attitudes, the mastery of perspective, the feeling for nature, and the insertion of antique elements into the picture.*

oil) and applied them to a wooden block or a stretched canvas. Since oil dries slowly, the artist was able to correct details or remove them. The new technique and the use of varnish allowed the painter to render the tiniest nuances of light or of light and shade, so well illustrated by the sfumato of Leonardo da Vinci, who liked to leave the background of his paintings in a kind of fine mist.

From Craftworker to Artist

In the fifteenth century, painters were considered by their sponsors to be no more than workers. In the account books of the princes who ordered paintings from them, painters ranked with plasterers, masons, and wheelwrights. Painters were craftworkers who, as the occasion demanded, accepted all kinds of work. They painted furniture, fashioned jewelry, and colored flags. Often they worked together, passing secrets of the trade among themselves. Their training was long, following the tradition of the blacksmith, the master clothier, or the saddler. In his *Book of Art*, Cennino Cennini, in the fifteenth century, traced the slow advance of a child who entered a famous master's workshop: "First of all, thou wilt need a year to study the elementary drawing that thou makest on thy tablets. To remain with the master in his shop, to make thyself acquainted with all the branches of our art—mixing the colors, cooking the pastes, kneading the plasters, making thyself skillful at preparing the panels and polishing them—for all this thou wilt need six years. Then

in order to study color, to make draperies of gold, and to break thyself into working on walls, thou wilt need another six years, always drawing, never leaving thy drawing, whether it be workday or feast."

In a few decades, although his training remained basically the same, the artist's place in society changed. He became a personage—just as important, just as esteemed as the scholar, the philosopher, or the humanist. Michelangelo, Raphael, Titian, Leonardo, and Dürer were admired by popes, kings, and emperors. There were stories that Emperor Charles V bent down one day to pick up Titian's paintbrush and that Francis I was present at Leonardo's deathbed. Legends no doubt, but surely significant of the glory of the greatest men of the Renaissance.

Women and Children During the Renaissance

In The Grandfather and His Grandson *(The Louvre), the Florentine painter Domenico Ghirlandajo expressed all the tenderness uniting a grandfather and his grandchild, in a scene revealing the new emphasis by artists on the world of children.*

reached thirty, victim of a common sickness or an epidemic or of unruly soldiers passing through the village. So the death of children, like that of adults, was considered to be determined by the hand of fate and was accepted as an event so frequent as to be almost normal. In the seventeenth century, Montaigne wrote: "I have lost two or three suckling children, not without regret, but without being much disturbed."

A New Kind of Teaching

In the middle-class circles of the towns, at the princely courts, in the castles of the aristocracy, and in places where daily life was less difficult, feelings toward children developed. Attachment to children grew. Children touched the hearts of their parents and grandparents. One sign of this change was that, in religious paintings the infant Jesus took on the features of a real child, whereas before he was always given the severe face of an adult, sometimes even a face with wrinkles. Plans were made, too, to give children a new kind of education. The demands of scholarship grew considerably, and discipline, unheard of in the Middle Ages, was introduced into the colleges and universities. The study day was divided into lessons of two or three hours, one after another, from dawn to dusk, with a short interruption for lunch. The teaching of good manners was not neglected. In a book printed in 1555, children are advised "not to attend to their needs in public, not to sneeze too much, to avoid yawning too often in front of other people, and not to eat like a glutton."

Erasmus himself, in his treatise *The Manners of Children,* recommends that they not have dirty

Family life as we know it today was born in the Renaissance. But at first this evolution concerned only the most privileged classes of society. In the countryside nothing changed to any great extent. There the harshness of everyday life gave people little time to concern themselves with the fate of others. Work in the fields, the daily struggle to avoid the pain of hunger, and fear of the morrow occupied mind and body. Often death cut down one or several children in the same family. The father and mother might also disappear by the time he or she noses, laugh at obscene words or gestures, or cheat at games. He points out that "blowing one's nose with one's cap, or on the hem of his coat, is the habit of a peasant, doing it with the arm or the elbow is that of a salt provision dealer. It is not much better to blow the nose with the hand and then wipe the hand on one's clothes. It is more proper to use a handkerchief."

Women of Character

The Renaissance, being less coarse, more civil, and more attuned to the needs of children than the Middle Ages was, also took into consideration the place of women in society. Certainly women remained under the control of their fathers or husbands. They were married at about fourteen years of age, often without being asked their opinion. Nevertheless, they did achieve a certain amount of liberty in the fifteenth and sixteenth centuries, which were not lacking in great feminine personalities.

Isabella d'Este in Ferrara set the tone of one of the most brilliant courts of the Italian Renaissance. Margaret of Navarre, elder sister of Francis I, surrounded herself with writers and artists. In Rome, Vittoria Colonna wrote magnificent religious poetry, and Louise Labé wrote verses that were rather profane. In tune with this new consideration for women the French poet Brantôme judged that women were nearer to God than men were because "they more resembled the divinity than we do, because of their beauty; for what is beautiful is nearer to God, Who is beauty itself, than ugliness which belongs to the devil." Sometimes an opposite evaluation took place, and women went to the stake because they possessed the beauty

of the devil. Certainly some judges did not share Brantôme's opinion.

It was in the middle-class circles of the cities that a true form of equality between husband and wife began to develop. Both were usually drawn from the same class of merchants, traders, or bankers. The husband owned the shop or studio, but the wife brought her dowry, her

housewifely skills, and a knowledge of business acquired in her own family. In the absence of her husband, she helped to run the business, or she took it over if she was left a widow.

Thus, the role of women changed during the Renaissance—in the courtly celebrations, in the literary groups, and in middle-class homes.

Many painters portrayed couples from the banking and money-changing professions. Here the Flemish painter Quentin Massys, in The Banker and His Wife *(The Louvre), underlines the economic role of the wife who, in certain circles, achieved a form of equality with her husband—if only because she had also brought him a comfortable dowry.*

Elsewhere in the World

Europe, between 1450 and 1550, was developing a civilization that would soon envelop the whole world. But everywhere, on different continents, cultures and ways of life were growing, far from being overturned by the arrival of the first European traders and navigators. The great exception was in America, where the Inca and Aztec empires disappeared.

The First Czar

The sixteenth century saw the real birth of Russia, around the large principality of Moscow. In the reign of Ivan III, Moscow became the capital of a vast country that believed itself to be heir to the Byzantine Empire after the fall of Constantinople. In the sixteenth century, as if to better illustrate this role, Ivan IV, called Ivan the Terrible, assumed the title of *czar* on his accession to the throne in 1557 and declared his intention of becoming the Caesar of a new Eastern empire.

Suleiman the Magnificent

The first decades of the sixteenth century were among the most brilliant periods in the history of the Ottoman Empire. During the reign of Sultan Suleiman II, known as Suleiman the Magnificent, from 1520 to 1566, the Turks extended their domination in the East as far as India and in the West to the gates of Vienna. But the sultan was not just a conqueror. He took care of the administration of his possessions, did not disdain poetry, and spent time on the beautification of

Equipped with sabers, armor and helmets that are genuine works of art, the great lords of Japan waged a fratricidal struggle.

the cities of his vast empire. This empire suffered its final great setback five years after the death of Suleiman, when the fleet of the united Christian powers crushed the Ottoman squadrons at the battle of Lepanto in 1571.

The China of the Ming Dynasty

In the fifteenth and sixteenth centuries, the huge Chinese empire was ruled by the Ming dynasty. Peking became the capital in 1450, and the country made great strides agriculturally, commercially, and in the area of arts and crafts. New plants, such as corn and sweet potatoes, were brought from America by European traders and were gradually accepted. China experienced the beginnings of a tremendous demographic expansion, which made her go from 60 million inhabitants in 1400 to 150 million in 1600.

The Japan of the Daimyos

In spite of incessant civil wars waged by the daimyos, the great lords, Japan was in a period of full economic and cultural expansion. Commerce flourished while several traits characteristic of Japanese civilization developed. These were the No theater, the art of the garden, and the refinement of the tea ceremony.

The Great Mogul

Akbar, a distant descendant of Tamerlane and Genghis Khan, reigned over a vast empire in India between 1542 and 1565. This Indian empire saw the height of a Hindu-Muslim civilization made possible by religious tolerance and marked by development of the arts, sciences, and technology.

The Songhai Empire

Centered on the Niger River, the great Songhai Empire, the most powerful Muslim state in black Africa, was formed at the end of the fifteenth century. Thanks to agriculture, stock farming, gold mines, and the caravan trade coming from Morocco and Egypt, the cities of Gao, Tombouctou, and Djenné emerged. They were not only merchant cities but also active intellectual and religious centers.